La Celestina: A Feminist Reading of the Carpe Diem

Scripta Humanistica

Directed by
BRUNO M. DAMIANI
The Catholic University of America

ADVISORY BOARD

La Celestina: A Feminist Reading of the Carpe Diem

Diane Hartunian

𝔖cripta 𝔥umanistica
75

La Celestina: A Feminist Readi ɪg of the carpe diem theme/ Diane Hartunian

    p. cm. — (Scripta Humanistica; 75)

    Includes bibliographical references

ISBN 0-816379-81-7 : $45.50

1. Rojas, Fernando de, d. 1541. Celestina. 2. Rojas, Fernando de, d. 1541 — Technique.
3. Pleasure in literature. I. Title. II. Title: Carpe diem theme. III. Series: Scripta
Humanistica (series) ; 75.

PQ6428.H37   1992

862'.2--dc20

                                              92-8880

                                                 CIP

Publisher and Distributor:

Scripta Humanistica

1383 Kersey Lane

Potomac, Maryland 20854

U.S.A.

To my father, in memory

Acknowledgements

I am most grateful to Professor Bruno Mario Damiani for his constant encouragement and inspiration. I am equally endebted to Professor Joseph Snow of the Michigan State University for his generous assistance concerning my work on *Celestina*. Special thanks to Professors Enrique Rodríguez-Cepeda and to Dr.Yvette Flores-Ortiz for their suggestions and encouragement.

Contents

Just as Fernando de Rojas was aware of the ambiguous nature of his work and the contradictory interpretations it might inspire, so Diana Hartunian recognizes that her own analysis is more apt to generate discussion than to provide a definitive feminist reading of La Celestina. This is to her credit. Critics such as Hartunian and Mary S. Gossy (whose The Untold Story: Women and Theory in Golden Age Texts came out in 1990, the same year that Hartunian completed the preliminary version of this study) are opening new doors for generations of scholars by questioning commonly held assumptions about male authority in Renaissance and Golden Age literature. Hartunian cites studies such as Bakhtin's Rabelais and His World and Paul Julian Smith's Writing in the Margin to show that both critic and text are part of a shifting process. No text is fixed and no interpretation is conclusive; text and reader are engaged in an endless dialectic. Perhaps no work illustrates this better that La Celestina, which has been the subject of conflicting interpretations for five hundred years.

Hartunian's contribution is a distinctly feminist analysis of La Celestina, in which she argues that while traditional carpe diem literature is misogynistic, Celestina's carpe diem message is androgynous. Hartunian asserts that in spite of exhorting women to enjoy their youth, poets such as Garcilaso and Góngora use carpe diem to denigrate women and reduce them to nothingness; in male-centered Renaissance poetry the poet becomes a spectator who watches a woman's demise and derives a message from it. In contrast, Celestina's _carpe diem_ call elevates women because it puts them on an equal footing with men. The bawd incites women as well as men to enjoy youth and carnal pleasure, for time passes for both. If, as countless moralists affirm, the fresh beauty of young women will soon fade, so too will the grace and vigor of young men.

One may disagree with Hartunian's conclusion that by displacing the authority of the _carpe diem_ caller from a male to a female character, Rojas converts _carpe diem_ into "a political call of persuasion destined to women to liberate themselves from the patriarchal system..." After all, both Celestina and Melibea come to a bad end. (Does an evil, male-dominated society punish them for daring to break out of the mold of subservience and dependence or does the author punish them for their immorality? Or both? Or neither?) Still, one must recognize that for the first time in the history of Spanish literature, the author of _La Celestina_ creates robust, multi-faceted, autonomous, self-reliant female characters who celebrate pleasure and act according to their own inclinations, consciously rejecting the social norms of their day. By focusing on Celestina's call of _carpe diem_, to which Melibea responds whole-heartedly, Hartunian sheds new light on the complexity and possible subversiveness of _La Celestina_.

Taking as a point of departure Derrida's view that in Western metaphysics the male is always the center of reference, Hartunian builds her arguments on a strong foundation of feminist theory. Citing critics such as Barbara Johnson, Toril Moi, and Mary Ellman, she reiterates that the two primary tasks of feminist criticism are the deconstruction of a male-dominated, patriarchal Western culture that has marginalized women and the reconstruction of Western culture from a feminine perspective. Hartunian relies heavily on the French feminists, who, unlike their American counterparts, extol femininity, rather than striving for equality with men. This celebration of feminine values, outlooks, sense and sensuality is pertinent to Hartunian's thesis because it is her view that the female characters in La Celestina develop and progress distinctly as women, "both in their character development and their ideologies."

The fact that these characters were created by a man is insignificant. Hartunian agrees with Hélène Cixous that the gender of the author does not determine whether or not a work is feminist. She asserts that "Feminist readings of works written by some male authors, as is the case with Rojas, reveal images of positive, non-denigrating women characters" and concludes that "these works are thus supportive of feminist theories."

Hartunian has written a provocative, intelligent book that is certain to generate debate. It is a fitting tribute to La Celestina, a masterwork that has continued to enthrall the reader and stimulate analysis for five centuries.

Barbara Mujica
Georgetown University

Introduction

The classical literary theme known as *carpe diem* or *seize the day*, is one of great popularity both in classical and Renaissance literature. The *carpe diem* theme stresses the enjoyment of present pleasures in fear of the brevity of life and the finality of death: "Be wise, decant the wine, prune back your long-term hopes. Life ebbs as I speak: so seize each day, and grant the next no credit."[1] Most frequently found in Spanish Golden Age lyric poetry, the *carpe diem* theme is also an essential literary theme of Golden Age prose. Among numerous works in Golden Age prose containing the *carpe diem* theme is *Celestina*, (Fernando de Rojas, 1499), a novel of particular interest for its structural, stylistic, and ideological dependence on this literary theme.

The purpose of this monograph is to examine the functions of the *carpe diem* theme in *Celestina*. In the course of my study, I show how the *carpe diem* theme reveals itself as the *prime mover* of virtually all aspects of the novel including characterization and plot development, stylistic aspects, and its ideological intentions.

Although attention has been given to the presence of the *carpe diem* theme in Spanish poetry, only scant references have been made to this theme in the prose of the Golden Age. Critical studies tend to treat only superficially this theme, which has been described as "one of the greatest traditional commonplaces of European literature."[2] Even though recognition has been given with respect to the importance of this theme in European literature, critics have largely overlooked its depth and impact on Spanish literature, and in particular to *Celestina*. To my knowledge, no critical analysis exists which examines exclusively the *carpe diem* theme either in Spanish prose or in *Celestina*, a literary masterpiece considered second in importance only to Cervantes' *Don Quixote.*

Chapter one offers an explanation of the *carpe diem* concept and the evolution of this centuries-old theme, which can be traced from Proverbs and the Wisdom of Solomon, to Hellenistic and Roman lyric poetry. In addition, the influence

---

[1]W.G. Shepherd, trans., *The Complete Odes and Epodes*, by Horace, (Middlesex: Peguin Books Ltd., 1983) 79; I.II.

[2]T.S. Eliot, *Selected Essays* (New York: Harcourt, Brace, and World, 1950) 253.

1

of Graeco-Roman writers on *Celestina* is analyzed with the intent of assessing the influence of this classical theme in Rojas' work.

Chapter two studies character portrayal as related to the *carpe diem* theme, which as we shall see, is the unifying force of both plot and character development, as it is expressed either directly or indirectly by almost all of the characters. I also show how the *carpe diem* acts as a catalyst in permitting the protagonist Celestina to persuade and convince others to follow her call to enjoyment. It is precisely by means of the *carpe diem* theme that each character achieves certain goals such as the amorous union of Calisto and Melibea, the erotic encounter of Pármeno and Areúsa, the monetary desires of Celestina, and the material pursuits of the servants Sempronio and Pármeno. *Seizing the day* transforms an inactive state, i.e., Calisto's initial desire for Melibea into an active realization.

The third chapter, titled *Stylistic Aspects*, focuses on the various stylistic devices that Rojas employs to communicate the *carpe diem* theme. This chapter attempts to show how Rojas' stylistic traits function as a catalyst to communicate effectively the *carpe diem* theme through language and literary artifice which distinguishes itself for its unique sensuality. A thorough analysis of *carpe diem* imagery, symbolism, metaphors, and other linguistic devices is carried out. The purpose of this chapter is to show how the *carpe diem* system of language and imagery in *Celestina* has its own unique verbs, metaphors, and vocabulary. The examination of such literary devices as the frequent use of verbs of enjoyment, graphically erotic visual descriptions of the human body and all its senses, temporal indicators, sexually oriented language, and erotically suggestive adages and proverbs, not only underscores the importance of the *carpe diem* theme, but reveals also the similarities that exist between the language and imagery of the *carpe diem* philosophy in *Celestina* and what Mikhail Bakhtin defines as the bodily lower stratum.

Chapter four discusses what is traditionally considered the most controversial aspect of *Celestina*: the diverse ideological implications of the novel. This chapter focuses on the ideological implications within the scope of the *carpe diem* theme. I show that a feminist reading of the *carpe diem* theme in *Celestina*, reveals a positive and liberating portrait of female characters. The application of certain contemporary French feminist theories such as those of Hélène Cixous and Luce Irigaray, helps elucidate how Rojas deconstructs and thus breaks with patriarchal attitudes towards women. This is typical of Spanish Golden Age *carpe diem* poetry where the male poet, despite his call to woman to enjoy, is the sole initiator and

2

recipient of the *carpe diem* call of persuasion to enjoy youth. The *carpe diem* call in *Celesitna* however, enables woman to experience *jouissance* as it serves as a catalyst for woman's repudiation of patriarchal values.

Chapter One

The *carpe diem* theme: A Historical and Literary Perspective

Celestina, written by Fernando de Rojas in 1499, is unquestionably one of Spain's most celebrated literary masterpieces. *Celestina* has enjoyed great popularity both in Spain and in other countries; this is reflected in the numerous translations of the work into several foreign languages, including German, French, Latin, Italian, English, Dutch, and most recently, Japanese.[3]

Considered by some critics as second in importance only to Cervantes' *Don Quixote*, *Celestina* has been the subject of diverse criticism.[4] Of perennial interest is the influence of *Celestina* on subsequent literature, which can be observed particularly in the development of literature in Spain between 1521 and 1554.[5] In addition, certain enigmatic aspects of the *Celestina*, such as its controversial authorship, its generic classification as either prose or drama, or both, and its multifaceted ideological intentions, have motivated critics to further research these diverse subjects.[6]

3 For a bibliography of *Celestina* see Joseph T. Snow, *Celestina by Fernando de Rojas: An Annotated Bibliography of World Interest 1930-1985* (Madison: The Hispanic Seminary of Medieval Studies, 1985). For an update of the above bibliography see Joseph T. Snow, ed., *Celestinesca* (Athens: U of Georgia, Dept. of Romance Languages, 1985-91). See also Erna Ruth Berndt-Kelly, "Peripecias de un título: En torno al nombre de la obra de Fernando de Rojas," *Celestinesca* 9 (Fall, 1985): 3-46. Concerning two recent translations of *Celestina* into Japanese see *Celestinesca* 12 (Mayo, 1988): 70.
4 Stephen Gilman, *The Spain of Fernando de Rojas: The Intellectual and Social Landscape of 'La Celestina'*. (Princeton: Princeton UP, 1972) 315.
5 *Celestina* served as a model for at least the following works: *La comedia Thebaida, La segunda comedia de Celestina, La tercera parte de la tragicomedia de Celestina, La tragicomedia de Lisandro y Rosalia, La tragedia policiana, La comedia llamada Florinea, La comedia Selvagia*; See Pierre Huegas, *'La Céléstine' et sa descendence directe* (Bordeaux: Institut d'Etudes Ibériques et Ibéro-Américaines de l'Université de Bordeaux, 1973).
6 Concerning the didactic intentions of *Celestina*, see Marcel Bataillon, *'La Célestine' selon Fernando de Rojas* (Paris: Didier, 1961); Vicente Cantarino, "Didactismo y moralidad de 'La Celestina,'" *ACTAS* 103-109; Dorothy C. Clarke, *Allegory, Decalogue and Deadly Sins in 'La Celestina'* Berkeley: U of California P, 1968); José Antonio Maravall, *El Mundo Social de 'La Celestina'* (Madrid: Gredos, 1964, 1968, 1972, 1976).

This study, however, will focus on an entirely different subject, an analysis of the classical literary theme known as *carpe diem*, and its influence and presence in *Celestina*. This ingeniously written work is of particular interest because of its thorough incorporation of this literary theme, in all its aspects -- structural, stylistic, and ideological.

The classical literary theme known as the *carpe diem* is one of great popularity, not only among classical and Renaissance writers, but by authors of all literary epochs. As Blanca González de Escandón, author of one of the principal studies of the *carpe diem* theme in Spanish poetry, comments: "La comparación de la belleza femenina con la rosa, pertenece a todos los tiempos y a todos los paises...."[7] Indeed, the impact of this motif on literature throughout the centuries has been acknowledged by great writers, among them T.S. Eliot, for instance, who describes the *carpe diem* theme as "...one of the greatest traditional commonplaces of European literature."[8] Widespread in all ages, the theme is truly a universal concept and reflects one of humankind's major philosophical preoccupations.[9]

This chapter will present a synthesis of various definitions of the *carpe diem* theme, followed by an explanation of the origins and evolutions of the theme and a synopsis of previous studies of the *carpe diem* theme in Spanish literature.

To a large extent, critics tend to treat the *carpe diem* theme superficially. Most definitions do not extend beyond the most obvious interpretation, "Eat, drink, and be merry for tomorrow you die."[10] The more profound significance of the *carpe diem* theme is generally overlooked.[11] Not only is the *carpe diem* theme rather complex; in addition, its definitions are extensive and have even been categorized into various different *carpe diem* strains.[12]

Although this theme can be found in many Graeco-Roman works, the celebrated phrase *carpe diem* has traditionally been attributed to Ode XI of the Roman poet Horace (65-8 B.C.): "Be wise, decant the wine, prune back your long-term hopes. Life ebbs as I speak: so seize each day (*carpe diem*), and grant the next

---

7 Blanca González de Escandón, *Los temas del carpe diem y la brevedad de la rosa en la poesía española* (Barcelona: Universidad de Barcelona, 1938) 9.
8 Eliot 253.
9 See Frederick H. Candelaria, "The *Carpe Diem* Motif in Early Seventeenth Century Lyric Poetry with Particular Reference to Robert Herrick," diss., U of Missouri, 1959, 47, 107; Bruce W. Wardropper, *Spanish Poetry of the Golden Age* (New York: Appleton-Century Crofts, 1971) 63.
10 Shepherd 79.
11 See James Ellis Wellington, "An Analysis of the *Carpe Diem* Theme in Seventeenth Century English Poetry (1590-1700)," diss., Florida State U, 1955, 1-2.
12 Wellington 2-4.

no credit."[13] Even though Horace was not the first to use this theme, his famed line is one of the most well-known early examples, and Horace also had a great impact on Renaissance writers, to the extent that he was viewed as the incarnation of the classical writer.[14]

Horace's influence reached Renaissance writers; Spain was no exception.[15] It was Horace's ability to integrate the *carpe diem* theme with other Graeco-Roman themes that inspired other writers. Therefore, the association of the *carpe diem* theme with Horace's Ode XI is usual. Reflecting on this theme, Bruce Wardropper comments:

> Man is born to die. But in between birth and
> death there is much to appreciate, much that
> is worth holding on to for as long as possi-
> ble. A great deal of poetry has been written
> about man's dilemma in a world of time; his
> distress at leaving this world only slightly
> tempered by his hope of attaining reality in
> heaven.[16]

As Wardropper and others have shown, the *carpe diem* theme can thus be seen as containing the following elements:

> The passing of time.
>
> 2. The uncertain transitory nature of life, youth and beauty.
>
> 3. As a result of 1) and 2), the advice of the poet is to enjoy life now.
>
> 4. An attempt to comprehend the existence of the human being in nature, the *carpe diem* is not merely a pessimistic and superficial concept,but rather a didactic and philosophical one. It reflects an eschatological problem.[17]
>
> 5. A scope which is cosmic in application.

Although Horace's Ode XI is the most commonly cited source of the *carpe diem* theme, it is not however, the most ancient. The *carpe diem* theme appears indirectly

---

13 Shepherd 79.
14 Escandón 38-39.
15 Consult Menéndez Pelayo, *Horacio en España* (Madrid, 1885).
16 Wardropper 75.
17 Wellington 8.

in an ancient Egyptian text, dated as early as 2200 B.C., which speaks of the need of *carpe diem* pleasures to compensate for the brevity of man's existence:

> Generations pass away and others go
> on since the times of the ancestors. . . .
> They that build buildings, their places
> are no more. What has been done with
> them?
> I have heard the words of (the past sages)
> Imhotep and Hardedef, with whose sayings
> men speak so much--(but) what are their
> places (now)? Their walls are crumbled, their
> places are non-existent, as if they had
> never been.
> No one returns from (over) there, so that he
> might tell us their disposition, that he
> might tell us how they are, that he might
> still our hearts until we (too) shall go to
> the place where they have gone. . . . [18]

Another ancient Mesopotamian source dates from approximately 2000 B.C. This is the Gilgamesh epic, derived from even older materials:

> Gilgamesh, where are you wandering?
> The life that you are seeking all around
> you will not find.
> When the gods created mankind
> they fixed Death for mankind,
> and held back Life in their own hands.
> Now you, Gilgamesh, let your belly be full!
> Be happy day and night,
> of each day make a party,
> dance in circles day and night!
> Let your clothes be sparkling clean,
> let your head be clean, wash yourself with
> water.
> Attend to the little one who holds onto your

---

18 Wellington 9.

hand,

let a wife delight in your embrace.

This is the (true) task of mankind (?).[19]

In addition, references to the *carpe diem* theme can be found in the writings of a school of philosophy called the Cyrenaic, founded in the fourth century B.C. by a pupil of Socrates.[20]

One aspect of the *carpe diem* theme can be cited from biblical sources as well: "El hombre nacido de mujer de días y harto de sinsabores que sale como una flor y es cortada."[21] Another passage from the Bible that mentions the *carpe diem* theme is found in Job. 14.[22] It appears again in the Wisdom of Solomon 2.8: "Let us crown ourselves with rosebuds before they be withered."[23]

However, the literature of the Graeco-Roman period marks the culmination of the *carpe diem* in ancient times. In Greek mythology, the *carpe diem* concept is symbolized by the rose and its mythological origins.[24] The rose is associated in Greek mythology with Aphrodite, also known as Venus, the goddess of sensual love and beauty. While the goddess arose from the high sea, the rose sprang from the earth, becoming the flower cherished by Bacchus and destined to reign over his feast. Hence, the association of wine and roses becomes a prevalent motif within classical literature.

Escandón explains the significance of Venus in relation to the *carpe diem* theme, as well as the series of symbols and myths, created from Greek mythology, that came to be associated with the *carpe diem*. Venus, comments Escandón, "llega a representar la vida de la Naturaleza, que se adormece en otoño y revive en primavera, y representa la juventud malograda-- la rosa se convierte en representación de la caducidad de la vida humana."[25] The rose, therefore, acquired a double, antithetical meaning: on the one hand, it symbolized spring, fecundity, youth, life, and sensuality, and on the other, sadness, aging, and death. Within the classical context, the *carpe diem* theme sprang from this metaphor of the

---

19 Taken from the Old Babylonian version of the *Gilgamesh*, Maureen Gallery Kovacs, trans. *The Epic of Gilgamesh* (Stanford: Stanford UP, 1989.) 85 note I.
20 Wellington 12.
21 Escandón 49.
22 Escandón 49-50.
23 Susan Gwendolyn Ellzey, "The Renaissance Rose," diss., Florida State U, 1973, 14, footnote 29.
24 See Marie-Joëlle Louison-Lassablière, "La symbolique florale dans la poésie amoureuse de 1570 à 1620," Thèse de troisième cycle, Université de Saint-Etienne, 1982; Charles Joret, *La rose dans l'antiquité et au moyen age* (Paris, 1892).
25 Escandon 10.

ephemerality of the rose. Escandón expresses the dual significance of the *carpe diem* and its relation to the rose metaphor theme in the following words:

> De aquí brota espontáneamente la idea:la vida presente, la del joven, es bella, fragante, brinda las promesas de la prima-vera y del amor, es como la de la misma rosa, que no resiste fresca la llegada de la noche;más allá está la vejez, el invierno, en el que cesa la alegría fecunda de la Naturalezay donde nos aguarda la muerte, la tiniebla: gocemos, pues, de este mayo de rosas, ya queno podemos evitar las nieves de diciembre ni la nada de sombras.[26]

One of the most important sources of the *carpe diem* can be found in the *Greek Anthology*. The *Greek Anthology* is important because Renaissance poets such as Robert Herrick, du Bellay, and Ronsard, and Spanish poets such as Garcilaso de la Vega and Luis de Góngora were inspired by the ancient poets represented in the collection. An exemplary poem from the *Greek Anthology* , written by Leonidas of Tarentun in the third century B.C., depicts the *carpe diem* theme in this manner:

> Knowing well that thou wast born mortal,
> lift up thy heart, taking thy pleasure in
> feasting. Once dead, no enjoyment shall be
> thine. For I, too, who ruled over great
> Ninevah, am dust. I have what I ate, and
> my wanton frolics and the joys I learnt
> in Love's company, but those many and rich
> possessions are left behind. This is wise
> counsel for men concerning life.[27]

Another poet to use this theme was Anacreon of Teos, who had many imitators dating from the fifth century B.C. Their poetry is marked by a tone of extreme pessimism and cynicism. Frequent themes in Anacreontic poetry are pleasure, love, and wine. Emphasis is on drinking as a form of amusement and as a consolation for life's transience. The following is a translation and adaptation of Anacreontic verse by the English Renaissance poet Philip Ayres (1638-1712), titled "To Himself":

> Then fetch more bottles, Boy, and charge
> us round
> We'll fall to Bacchus, victims on the ground
> Nor value what dull moralists have said, I'm

---

26 Escandon 11.
27 Wellington 42.

sure 'tis better to be drunk, than dead.[28]

The next major use of the *carpe diem* theme occurs in the poetry of Latin writers. The Roman poet Catullus (84-54 B.C.) and his imitators are equally important in this regard. Catullus' celebrated ode titled *Carmen V* symbolizes a culmination of the *carpe diem* theme, and served as a source of inspiration for writers of Western literature as well. This ode, the only one written by Catullus, indeed exemplifies the *carpe diem* theme and prefigures many elements of it in *Celestina*, particularly the graphic representation of erotic love, the emphasis on the senses-- especially the tactile sense, and the implied rejection of social conventions, namely marriage:

> COME, Lesbia, let us live and love,
>
> nor give a damn what sour old men say.
>
> The sun that sets may rise again
>
> but when our light has sunk into the earth,
>
> it is gone forever.
>
> Give me a thousand kisses,
>
> then a hundred, another thousand,
>
> another hundred
>
> and in one breath
>
> still kiss another thousand,
>
> another hundred.
>
> O then with lips and bodies joined
>
> many deep thousands;
>
> confuse
>
> their number,
>
> so that poor fools and cuckolds
>
> (envious even now) shall never learn our
>
> wealth and curse us
>
> with their
>
> evil eyes.[29]

The *carpe diem* theme can be found in other Graeco-Roman writers, such as Heliodorus (A.D. 220-250), in his *Aethiopica*.[30] Another author who employs the theme, is Achilles Tatius (second-third centuries A.D.) in his *Leucippe and*

---

28 Wellington 32.
29 Catullus, *Poems of Catullus* trans. Horace Gregory, (New York: Covici-Friede, 1931) 19.
30 Mikhail Bakhtin, *The Dialogic Imagination*, trans. Caryl Emerson and Michael Holquist, ed. Michael Holquist (Austin: U of Texas P, 1981) 86.

10

Clitophon. Mikhail Bakhtin comments on the free and easy attitude toward sex of the heroines in these works. An interesting parallel can be made here between Tatius' heroine and the female characters of *Celestina*, with their liberal ideas towards sex.

One last Roman writer of great singularity is Ausonius (A.D. 310-395), famed for his poetic essay, "De rosis nascentibus." [31] This poem describes a garden and a philosophical discussion with a maiden on the significance of roses and mortality. The poet offers *carpe diem* advice to the maid to pluck the flower of youth before it fades:

> So many things, so rare, so young,
> A day begat them, and a day will end.
> O Earth, to give a flower so brief a
> grace!
> As long as a day is long, so long the
> life of a rose.
> The golden sun a morning sees her born,
> And late at eve returning finds her old.
> Yet wise is she, that hath so soon to die
> And lives her life in some succeeding
> rose.
> O maid, while youth is with the rose and thee
> Pluck thou the rose: life is as swift for
> thee.[32]

The Renaissance poets and philosophers, like the classical authors, were preoccupied with the themes of the *carpe diem*, mortality, and the passing of time. Leonardo da Vinci, for example, speaks of the *carpe diem* theme in his works:

> Now you see that the hope and the desire of
> returning home and to one's former state
> is like the moth to the light, and that the
> man who with constant longing awaits with
> joy each new spring time, each new summer,
> each new month and each new year--
> deeming that the things he longs for are

---

31 Some attribute the poem to Ausonius, others claim it is anonymous. See Ellzey 20, footnote 43.
32 Evelyn B. White, trans., "De rosis nascentibus," by Ausonius, (Cambridge: Harvard UP, 1949) vol. II, 271.

ever too late in coming--
does not perceive that he is longing for
his own destruction. . . .[33]

Da Vinci refers to time with disdain:

O Time! consumer of all things; O envious
age! thou dost destroy all things and
devour all things with the relentless
teeth of years, little by litle in a slow
death. . . .[34]

Spanish Renaissance writers were not different from their English, French, and Italian counterparts in their use of the *carpe diem* theme. Not only were Spanish writers conscious of *carpe diem* motifs; in addition, they translated and rewrote *carpe diem* poetry from antiquity.[35] Spanish Baroque poets such as Quevedo, for example, translated numerous poems; Herrera translated "De Rosis Nascentibus"; and Góngora translated Horace's "Oda a Leuconoe" and "Ad Ligurinum." However, it was Garcilaso de la Vega who introduced the *carpe diem* theme in Spain in his Sonnet XXIII, titled "En tanto que de rosa y de azucena," an imitation of Horace's ode, "Ad Ligurinum."[36]

Numerous studies treat the presence of the *carpe diem* theme in English and French literature. However, fewer studies exist in Spanish. Critics such as Candelaria, Wellington, and Ellzey compare the *carpe diem* theme of antiquity with English and French Renaissance poems such as Herrick's "To the virgins; to make much of time"; Waller's "Go, lovely Rose"; Spencer's *Faerie Queene*; Ronsard's ode XVII, "Versons ces roses près du vin." Although due attention has been given to the presence of the *carpe diem* theme in Spanish poetry,[37] only scant references have been made to this theme in the prose of the Golden Age, and no critical analysis exists, to m y knowledge, that examines exclusively the *carpe diem* theme in *Celestina*.

---

33 Jean Paul Richter, *The Notebooks of Leonardo da Vinci* (New York: Dover Publications, 1970) vol. II, 290.

34 Richter 290.

35 Escandón 56. For additional information concerning the influence of Antiquity on the Middle Ages and the Renaissance see Ernst Curtius, *European Literature and the Latin Middle Ages* (Princeton: Princeton UP, 1953).

36 Escandón 57.

37 R.P. Calcraft, "The Carpe Diem Sonnets of Garcilaso de la Vega y Góngora," *Modern Language Review* 76 (1981): 332-337; Alexander Pilotti, "A Structural Analysis of Three Sixteenth Century Spanish *Carpe Diem* Sonnets," diss., U of Michigan, Ann Arbor, 1976; Antonio García Berrio, "Tipología textual de los sonetos clásicos españoles sobre el *carpe diem*," *Disposito* 3-4 (1978-79): 243-271.

One of the most complete analyses of the *carpe diem* theme in Spanish literature is found in the anthology already cited by Escandón. In her introductory study, Escandón traces the *carpe diem* theme from Graeco-Roman times to the Renaissance and Baroque period, and even to Latin-American poets such as Rubén Darío. Not even in that authoritative work do we find, however, a study of the *carpe diem* in *Celestina*.

Renaissance writers looked to the classics as their sources. It is not surprising, therefore, that the characters in *Celestina* use classical sources and make use of the *carpe diem* theme. Dorothy Severin refers to *Celestina* as a "... tapestry of literary allusion and quotation, [where] almost every speech is somehow indebted to a previous literary source."[38] The references to classical sources in *Celestina*, as well as the use of *carpe diem* motifs, indicate the possibility that Rojas was familiar with themes of antiquity, a point well made by Castro Guisasola[39] and Américo Castro, among others. Castro suggests, in fact, that Rojas displayed a notable interest in classical literature.[40]

Although scarce biographical data on Rojas is available, it is documented that he was familiar with the classics, as attested by his own inventory of the books in his library, among them works by Cicero, Seneca, Petrarca, Terence, Apuleius, and Boethius.[41] For the present study of *Celestina*, the concept of intertextuality, which requires that a text be read only in relation to other texts, becomes an important means of determining to what extent it is possible that Rojas was influenced by classical authors:

38 Dorothy Sherman Severin, *Tragicomedy and Novelistic Discourse in Celestina* (Cambridge: Cambridge UP, 1989) 21.
39 Florentino Castro Guisasola, *Observaciones sobre las fuentes literarias de La Celestina* (Madrid: Consejo Superior de Investigaciones Científicas, 1973 2nd ed. rpt of the Madrid, 1924 ed.); Alan D. Deyermond, *The Petrarchan Sources of La Celestina* (London: Oxford UP, 1961).
40 Américo Castro, *Santa Teresa y otros ensayos* (Madrid: Historia Nueva, 1929) 198, 206.
41 Stephen Gilman "The Spanish Writer, Fernando de Rojas," *Yearbook of the American Philosophical Society* (1961): 503-505; Fernando del Valle Lersundi, "Documentos referentes a Fernando de Rojas," *Revista de Filología Española* 12 (1925): 385-396; Fernando del Valle Lersundi, "Testamento de Fernando de Rojas, autor de 'La Celestina,'" *Revista de Filología Española* 16 (1929): 366-383; María Rosa Lida de Malkiel, *Dos obras maestras de la literatura española. 'El Libro de Buen Amor' y 'La Celestina* '(Buenos Aires: Editorial Universitaria de Buenos Aires, 1966) 14, 106-7; Amancio Fernández Labandeira, "En torno a Fernando de Rojas y su biblioteca," in *Homenaje a Luis Morales Oliver,* (Madrid: Fundación Universitaria Española, 1986) 189-220; for the influence of Seneca on *Celestina* see Louise Fothergrill-Payne, *Seneca and 'La Celestina,* (Cambridge: Cambridge UP, 1988).

literary works are to be considered not as autonomous entities, 'organic wholes,' but as intertextual constructs: sequences which have meaning in relation to other texts which they take up, cite, parody, refute, or generally transform.[42]

In conclusion, Rojas was indeed familiar with the classics, and was with the *carpe diem* theme also. Not only is the *carpe diem* theme present in *Celestina*, as the present study will demonstrate; but this theme in fact provides important underlying structures for our appreciation of the form and meaning of the work. Not only does Rojas develop the theme through stylistic devices just as in poetry, but the *carpe diem* is depicted through characterization, stylistic devices and ideological intentions. Thus, in *Celestina*, Rojas adds several innovative manifestations to the *carpe diem* theme.

---

[42] Jonathan Culler *The Pursuit of Signs: Semiotics, Literature, Deconstruction.* (Ithaca: Cornell UP, 1981) 38.

14

Chapter Two

The Presence of the *carpe diem* theme in *Celestina*

Fernando de Rojas anticipated the Renaissance movement, including its literary, ideological and sociological implications, by capturing the very essence of this epoch in *Celestina.*[43] Indeed, Rojas, like other great writers of the Renaissance, such as Cervantes, Shakespeare, and Rabelais, depicts in *Celestina* the transition from the Dark Ages.

The French humanist François Rabelais posed the following question in a letter of 1532 to his friend, the magistrate Tiranqueau:

> ¿Cómo sucedió, sapientísimo Tiranqueau, que en la grandísima iluminación del gran tiempo presente, en el que vemos rehabilitados todos los mejores estudios por una singular y casi divina bendición, se encuentren en cualquier parte personas afectadas extrañamente que no pueden o no quieren apartar sus ojos de la densa y más que Cimerea oscuridad de los tiempos góticos hacia la brillante luz del sol?[44].

With these words Rabelais characterizes the Renaissance as a time of experimentation and rediscovery. Symbolized in the above passage by "la brillante luz del sol," the Renaissance virtually "bade farewell to the darkness of the Gothic ages."[45] The literary works of the Renaissance were a reflection of this transition: "Literary as well as other documents of that period prove a clear and carefully defined awareness of a great turning point, of a radical change of historical epochs."[46]

As humankind turned toward "la luz brillante del sol," it ceased to perceive the world from a theocentric perspective or to be preoccupied with the medieval concept

43 See Chapter Seven titled "Fernando de Rojas as Autjor", in Stephen Gilman, *The Spain of Fernando de Rojas* 355-390.
44 Cited by Bruno Mario Damiani, *Moralidad y didactismo en el Siglo de Oro* (Madrid: Orígenes, 1987) 11 from François Rabelais, *Oeuvres Complètes*, ed. Jacques Boulanger and Lucien Scheler (Paris: Gallimard, 1955) 954.
45 Mikhail Bakhtin, *Rabelais and His World*, trans. Hélène Iswolsky (Bloomington: Indiana UP, 1984) 98.
46 Bakhtin, *Rabelais* 98.

of *memento mori*. A transition took place away from the theocentric or "upward" focus of the Middle Ages, as defined by Mikhail Bakhtin (*Rabelais and His World*), to a homocentric emphasis or "downward" movement towards earthly concerns.[47] Consequently, two distinctive yet interdependent features typical of the Renaissance can be observed in the literature of the period. First, as mentioned above, a tendency towards experimentation and creation; and second, a rediscovery of classical antiquity, esteemed a truly humanistic movement of "studia humanitatis."

Not only did humankind rediscover the world, but also this "downward" movement focused on the human being as an individual; a growing self-consciousness occurred. Epitomizing this new movement is the following description of a Renaissance writing:

> On a donc vu dans l'écriture une activité positive et créatrice à l'intérieur de laquelle certains êtres parviennent a coincider pleine-ment avec eux-mêmes...L'élaboration d'une grande oeuvre littéraire n'est rien d'autre en effet que la découverte d'une perspective vraie sur soi-même, la vie, les hommes. Et la littérature est une aventure d'être.[48]

Self-consciousness triggered emphasis on the senses and on sensuality. It is not surprising, therefore, that there was a resurgence of the classical *carpe diem* concept of "seize the day" in Renaissance literature, which can be classified as a part and subsequently the result of the downward movement as defined by Bakhtin.[49] Spain was no exception to the Renaissance movement. Spanish works such as *La lozana andaluza, Lazarillo de Tormes, La pícara Justina*, and *Don Quixote*, are examples of the new literature of the Renaissance.[50]

Celestina is, in fact, an eminent reflection of the sensuality of the Renaissance being. Indeed, both Gilman and Lida describe the "sensual awareness of the work."[51] Even Rojas expresses in the prologue to his *Celestina* a particular interest in the erotic aspect of the lovers, in the process of the characters' delight, rather than just a concern for portrayal of two lovers.[52]

---

47 Bakhtin, *Rabelais* 21 "...the upper part is the face or the head and the lower part is the genital organs, the belly, and the buttocks."
48 Jean-Pierre Richard, *Littérature et Sensation* (Paris: Edition du Seuil, 1954) 14.
49 Bakhtin, *Rabelais* 1-58.
50 For the influence of *Celestina* on Renaissance literature see Pierre Huegas, 1973.
51 Stephen Gilman, *The Art of 'La Celestina '*(Madison: U of Wisconsin P, 1956) 10; Lida. *La originalidad.*
52 Fernando de Rojas, *La Celestina*, ed. Bruno Mario Damiani, 8th ed. (Madrid: Cátedra, 1980) 47-51. Henceforth all parenthetical references in my text refer to this edition, unless otherwise specified.

16

The process of the characters' passion is readily evident in the summary of the plot, which precedes the first act:

> Calisto fue de noble linaje, de claro ingenio, de gentil disposición, de linda crianza, dotado de muchas gracias, de estado mediano. Fue preso en el amor de Melibea mujer moza, muy generosa, de alta serenísima sangre sublimada en próspero estado, una sola heredera a su padre Pleberio, y de su madre Alisa muy amada. Por solicitud del pungido Calisto, vencido el casto propósito de ella, entreviniendo Celestina, mala y astuta mujer, con dos sirvientes del vencido Calisto, engañados y por ésta tornados desleales, presa su fidelidad con anzuelo de codicia y de deleite, vinieron los amantes y los que ministraron, en amargo y desastrado fin. Para comienzo de lo cual dispuso el adversa fortuna lugar oportuno, donde a la presencia de Calisto se presentó la deseada Melibea. (52)

The uniqueness of *Celestina* resides, in part, precisely in its complete reconstruction of the *carpe diem* theme. It is the use of the *carpe diem* theme as a tool of persuasion by the protagonist Celestina, and subsequently by the other characters, which gives the work an innovative quality. The degree to which this theme is developed is such that it can be considered the unifying force of characterization.[53] This chapter will treat characterization, body concepts, and the importance of eating and drinking in *Celestina*. All these subjects are directly related to the classical theme of the *carpe diem*.

In regard to character portrayal, the *carpe diem* theme is manifest on almost every page of *Celestina*, expressed directly or indirectly by almost all fourteen characters. Gilman, in *The Art of La Celestina*, comments:

> All along *Celestina* there occur and reoccur discussions of old age and youth, servitude and freedom, the opposing advantages of riches and poverty and the nature of men and women, discussions which are rooted in the preocupation of each individual with his conditioning.[54]

Although *Celestina* has been the subject of criticism, accused of a lack of characterization,[55] to assume that there is a lack of characterization in the work

---

53 See Erna Ruth Berndt-Kelly, *Amor, muerte y fortuna en 'La Celestina,,'*Madrid: Gredos, 1963) 46,97: "Esta prisa por vivir y este deseo de gozar de la juventud lo manifiestan todos los personajes en la obra de Rojas... Así la vida en *La Celestina* adquiere notas epicúreas. Celestina da por supuesto que el mayor bien y provecho del hombre es el deleite; es el placer."

54 Gilman, *The Art of 'La Celestina'* 59.

55 Gilman, *The Art of 'La Celestina,'*"56, 72-74. He resolves this problem of a "lack of fixed portraiture" by placing characterization within the framework of the dialogue.

would imply a misunderstanding of the creative innovations of Rojas. An examination of character portrayal in *Celestina* reveals, in fact, that the component parts of the *carpe diem* theme produce radical changes in the characters. These changes or transformations in turn form an integral part of the *carpe diem* theme. This view is set forth by Sarah Gilhead:

> As concept, decision, and act, 'seizing the day' transforms a state characterized as inactive, wasted, empty, meaningless into a state characterized as active, fulfilling, purposive, and self-actualizing.[56]

All characters in *Celestina* share the common trait of sensuality. The sensual and erotic portrayal of the characters occupies such a central position that background information such as historical data, including the name of the city where the action of the work develops, and in-depth information on the characters has been omitted. Indeed, what is usually considered pertinent information concerning character portrayal-- for example, detailed physical descriptions -- for the most part is absent from *Celestina*. Even though Celestina, Melibea, and Calisto are described physically, other characters such as Areúsa, Elicia, and the servants, Pármeno and Sempronio, are described with far less detail.

Nevertheless, Rojas chooses to portray his characters dramatically, through comments made by other characters, and through extralinguistic devices such as their sensual body behavior. It is not a coincidence that *Celestina* contains the words "deleite," "gozar," and other similar expressions which are important in the overall stylistic fibre of the novel and which will be studied further in Chapter three. What counts here is not the past of the characters or the story itself, but the present, and how the characters achieve maximum pleasure.[57] The characters are portrayed not only through their sensuality but through what Mikhail Bakhtin defines as the bodily lower stratum. They express themselves through body language, their clothes, and festivities in which wine and food are featured. Indeed, *Celestina* is a portrayal of the "gallery of sentiment of love."[58] The characters in *Celestina* need no justification of their origins or presence; they are worried about "aquí y ahora." In pursuit of the *carpe diem* theme, they reject all social conventions such as marriage (to be discussed further in Chapter four).

---

56 Sarah Gilhead, "Ungathering 'Gather ye Rosebuds': Herrick's Misreading of the '*Carpe Diem*,' *Criticism* 27 (1985): 133-134.
57 For a study of the importance of the past in *Celestina*, see Severin *Memory* 1970
58 Gilman, *The Art of 'La Celestina*.' 7.

18

Celestina has often been criticized both by contemporaries of Rojas and by early modern critics for its erotic and sometimes obscene passages and licentious portrayal of characters.[59] Despite the negative criticism of the "licentious" nature of Celestina, no one will disagree that Rojas achieved an unusually plausible, dynamic, complex portrayal of the characters. Through the technique of "perspectivism," Rojas presents a creative, modern version of the same carpe diem theme used since antiquity. Perspectivism is the portrayal of characters as described by the characters themselves. The characters define themselves and other characters through what Gilman defines as an interchange, between the "tú y yo," and through the structural form of the dialogue.[60] In Celestina, there is no third person narrator, except in the plot and act summaries. It is precisely by means of perspectivism, and the emphasis on the "tú y yo," that the carpe diem is so vividly and dynamically expressed. In Celestina, the characters depend on each other, they reflect and speak about each other, they "create" each other.

Another common feature of the characters of Celestina, in addition to their sensuality, is their individualism: "el rasgo sobresaliente de los personajes es su individualidad."[61] The reader perceives the highly sensual tone of Celestina through the free and open manner in which the characters express themselves. They do not hide feelings, especially concerning their sexuality; they depict passion as their most important raison d'être. Rojas' portrayal of characters makes use of what Bakhtin defines as the "lower bodily stratum," where the emphasis in a literary work is on sex, food, wine.

The principal character who manifests the carpe diem theme is the protagonist, the "mala y astuta mujer," Celestina.[62] Ramiro de Maeztu depicts Celestina as an interpreter of Satanic and hedonistic wisdom. Lida describes Celestina as a genius with "rápida inteligencia, don de improvisación para situaciones difíciles y domina los personajes."[63] Indeed, Celestina, described in the text itself as a "mala

---

59 See Juan de Valdés, Diálogo de la lengua, ed. José F. Montesinos, 6th ed. (Madrid: Espasa-Calpe, S.A., 1976) 182-183 For a more recent edition, see Cristina Barbolani, Madrid: Cátedra, 1982.
60 Gilman, The Art of 'La Celestina,'"57-58.
61 Lida, Dos obras 97.
62 Juan David García Bacca, "Sobre el sentido de 'conciencia' en La Celestina," Revista de Guatemala 6 (1946): 52-66. He claims that Celestina is the central figure.
63 Ramiro de Maeztu, La Celestina, o el saber, ,Don Quijote, Don Juan and La Celestina: ensayos de simpatía (Madrid: Ed. Calpe, 1926); Lida Dos Obras 70; see Catherine Swietlicki, "Rojas' View of Women: A Reanalysis of La Celestina," Hispanófila I, (1985): 1-13; "It is Rojas' characterization of Celestina of course, which is most remarkable. By perfecting attributes drawn from several literary antecedents, Celestina's creator has

y astuta mujer" (52), represents what would be the equivalent of the poet in *carpe diem* poetry. She is the "prima mobile," who by means of her *carpe diem* arguments, convinces, persuades, and transforms the others. She invites youth-- Calisto, Melibea, Pármeno, Areúsa, Sempronio, and Elicia, and Lucrecia to enjoy life. Throughout the novel there are exhortations to enjoyment issued by Celestina similar to the following: "gocémonos y aprovechémonos, que sobre el partir nunca reñiremos"(132). Celestina herself sets forth the *carpe diem* example "asi goze de esta alma pecadora." Thus the *carpe diem* acts as a catalyst permitting Celestina to persuade and convince the characters to enjoy life; it is through Celestina's *carpe diem* persuasions that the erotic union of Calisto and Melibea takes place.

In the first act, Celestina gives her definition of *carpe diem*; she has what may be perceived as a *carpe diem* school of philosophy comparable to the "escuela de buscones" in Quevedo's picaresque novel *El Buscón*. The first *carpe diem* call occurs when Celestina persuades Sempronio to join her: "...que los bienes, si no son comunicados, no son bienes.Ganemos todos, partamos todos, holguemos todos"(79). The essence of the Celestinesque *carpe diem* theme is expressed in the verbs "ganar," "holgar," "aprovechar," and "gozar." Throughout the entire novel, in all the acts, the *carpe diem* call is reiterated-- thus reinforcing Celestina's arguments and the philosophical underpinnings of Rojas' view of life.

Within Celestina's *carpe diem* definition is the idea of sharing: "todo lo mío es tuyo" (act V)-- which reflects the aphorism, ". . . the good things in life must be shared to be enjoyed."[64] For Celestina, sharing encompasses the sharing of sensual carnal pleasures; for example, Celestina exclaims to Areúsa in Act VII:

> ...Por Dios, pecado ganas en no dar parte de estas gracias a todos los que bien te quieren. Que no te las dio Dios para que pasases en balde por la frescor de tu juventud...(162)

It also encompasses the sharing of friendship, as expressed by Celestina upon recalling her friend Claudina, Sempronio's mother:

> ...Su madre e yo, uña y carne; Juntas comíamos, juntas dormíamos, juntas habíamos nuestros solaces, nuestros placeres, nuestros consejos y conciertos. (102)

---

produced an original personage who is prostitute, procuress, necromancer, pharmacist, and mother figure." 5-6

64 For more on the ironic aspects of sharing see Henry Mendeloff, "Sharing in *La Celestina*," *Boletín del Instituto Caro y Cuervo* 32 (1977): 173-77; Gilman *The Art* 120-127; Rosa María Lida de Malkiel, *La Originalidad Artística de 'La Celestina,'* (Buenos Aires: Editorial universitaria de Buenos Aires, 1962) 252-254.

Along with the concept of sharing is the idea of experience, particularly sexual experience, as a positive element within the *carpe diem* theme; sexual experience rejuvenates and embellishes both women and men. As can be observed in the following poem by Asclepiades de Samos in the *Palatine Anthology*, this idea, too, can be traced to antiquity:

> ¿Quieres aguardar tu virginidad?
> ¿Qué conseguirás con eso?
> No es en los infiernos donde
> encontrarás un amante, muchacha.
> Entre los vivos se gozan los placeres
> de Cypris. En el imperio de Aqueronte,
> pobrecilla, no seremos ya sino hueso
> o ceniza.[65]

In *Celestina* and in the *carpe diem* tradition, the idea of loss of virginity equals a positive gain in experience. As Celestina says, it would be "sinful" not to enjoy: "Por Dios, pecado ganas en no dar parte de estas gracias a todos los que bien te quieren" (162). The view that men and women must pursue their sexual instincts is not only expressed by Celestina, it also forms an essential part of her technique of persuasion.[66] This is precisely how Celestina justifies the *carpe diem* theme and convinces the others, as we see when she attempts to convince Melibea: "...y la natura ordenóla Dios, y Dios no hizo cosa mala. . ." (129).[67] Celestina's technique of persuasion is so effective that the others later preach the same theme, as when Pármeno states, after his sexual encounter with Areúsa: "...Bien me decía la vieja que de ninguna prosperidad es buena la posesión sin compañía. El placer no comunicado no es placer" (172). Celestina's technique has already proved itself to be effective, since prior to her "case" with Calisto and Melibea, she is already well-known; everyone including the clergy and nobility remembers her.[68]

Celestina possesses god-like powers which give her an authoritative role. These powers are a reminder of the Renaissance anthropocentric conception of the human being as the most significant entity of the universe. Celestina is therefore the "love authority," as we see when Sempronio describes Celestina to Calisto:

---

65 Escandón 20.
66 Otis Handy, "The Rhetorical and Psychological Defloration of Melibea," *Celestinesca* 7 (1983): 17-27. Handy says that Act X is proof of Celestina's art of seduction.
67 Everett W. Hesse, "La función simbólica de la Celestina," *Boletín de la biblioteca Menéndez Pelayo* 42 (1966): 87-95.
68 See Dorothy Sherman Severin, *Memory in "La Celestina"* (London: Tamesis, 1970).

> Días ha grandes que conozco en fin de esta vecindad una vieja barbuda
> que se dice Celestina, hechicera, astuta, sagaz en cuantas maldades hay;
> entiendo que pasan de cinco mil virgos los que se han hecho y deshecho
> por su autoridad en esta ciudad.(68)

The authoritative role that Celestina enjoys is part of the *carpe diem* theme also, for it is precisely as issuer of the *carpe diem* summons that Celestina wields authority.[69] Through Celestina's "auditory autonomy,"[70] she is able to convince the others of the "glorification of physical pleasures as man's only consolation for a vain and transitory existence."[71]

It has been stated that Celestina's technique of persuasion is so successful that not only does she convince Melibea to unite with Calisto, but she also passes the *carpe diem* theme onto her followers. After Celestina's death, for example, Areúsa says: "...Que cuando una puerta se cierra, otra suele abrir la fortuna..." (256). Areúsa employs the same techniques of persuasion and preaches the *carpe diem* theme in that she celebrates more the pleasure of life than the lamentation of death.

The *carpe diem* serves, therefore, as a catalyst in *Celestina*, and the protagonist, Celestina, is indeed the "prima mobile" of the novel. It is through her *carpe diem* philosophy that she is able to persuade the other characters to seize the day. Among the other characters who play an important role in the development of the *carpe diem* theme, Calisto is portrayed as a concupiscible lover, even though initially his rhetoric and behavior appear to fall within the courtly tradition.[72] For example, Calisto is described in the "argumento general" as being of

> ...noble linaje, de claro ingenio, de gentil disposición, de linda crianza, dotado de muchas gracias de estado mediano.

Calisto's first encounter with Melibea also fits into the courtly tradition, although Melibea is offended by his terms of appraisal:

> En esto veo, Melibea, la grandeza de Dios ...En dar poder a natura que de tan perfecta hermosura te dotase, y hacer a mí inmérito tanta merced que verte alcanzase... 53-54)

He even places Melibea before God:

---

69 Berrio 250.
70 Gilman, *The Art* 12.
71 Wellington 55.
72 Inés Azar, "Metáfora, literalidad, transgresión: Amor-Muerte en *La Celestina* y en la Egloga II de Garcilaso," *Lexis* 3 (July 1979): 57-65; See Alan D.Deyermond, "The Text-Book Mishandled: Andreas Capellanus and the Opening Scene of *La Celestina*." *Neophilologus* 45 (1961): 218-21; June Hall Martin, *Love's Fools; Aucassin, Troilus, Calisto and the Parody of the Courtly Lover*. (London: Támesis, 1972.)

¿Yo? Melibeo soy y a Melibea adoro y en Melibea creo y a Melibea amo. (56)

Calisto has thus rejected Christian concepts for a pagan idolization of Melibea. He is completely obsessed with "bienes mundanos":

...oh bienes mundanos, indignos de ser poseídos de tan alto corazón...(78)

Calisto even perceives pleasure when he dreams of Melibea; completely obsessed with the *carpe diem* theme, he repeatedly uses forms of the terms "gozar" and "deleitar":

...En mis brazos te tengo y no lo creo. Mora en mi persona tanta turbación de placer, que me hace no sentir todo el gozo que poseo. (242)

Calisto differs from the other characters in that he is the only one who does not need to be transformed by Celestina. It is Melibea who transforms him; she stirs his *carpe diem* desire.[73] This transformation of Calisto by Melibea can be observed indirectly through the episodes that mention the "cordón." This device, with which Celestina convinces Melibea, is the same device that serves as a catalyst to intensify even further Calisto's desire for Melibea:

...Y mándame mostrar aquel santo cordón, que tales miembros fue digno de ceñir. ¡Gozarán mis ojos con todos los otros sentidos, pues juntos han sido apasionados! (144)

Lida describes Calisto as "débil," "quejoso," "sentimental," and "egoísta."[74] Calisto is obsessed with his own enjoyment: he seems to be even more preoccupied about his own destiny after learning of the deaths of Celestina, Sempronio, and Calisto:

¿Qué será de mí? ¿Adónde iré? ¿Qué salga allá? A los muertos no puedo ya remediar ...(239)

On the other hand, Calisto's monologue in Act XIV reveals a more profound, philosophical side. He is well aware of his actions and their consequences, but perceives himself as a victim of circumstances:

¡Oh breve deleite mundano: cómo duran poco y cuestan mucho tus dulzores! No se compra tan caro el arrepentir!... (247)

---

73 Virginia H.Boullosa, "La concepción del cuerpo en *La Celestina*," in *La idea del cuerpo en las letras españolas (siglo XIII a XVII)*, ed. Dinko Cvitanovic, (Bahía Blanca, Argentina: Univ. Nacional del Sur, 1973), 88-117, 94: "Calisto despierta a la vida sensual con la transformación de su cuerpo, obrada por la visión de Melibea."
74 Lida *La Originalidad* 57.

Melibea

Juan de Valdés comments on Melibea

> Marcio.-- ¿Qué personas os parecen que están mejor esprimidas?
>
> Valdés.-- La de Celestina está a mi ver per- fetíssima en todo quanto pertenece a una fina alcahueta, y las de Sempronio y Pármeno; la de Calisto no stá mal, y la de Melibea pudiera estar mejor.
>
> Marcio.-- ¿Adonde?
>
> Valdés.-- Adonde se dexa muy presto vencer, no solamente a amar pero a gozar del deshonesto fruto del amor.
>
> Marcio.--Tenéis razón.[75]

Valdés and Marcio are both in agreement on what may be considered a highly perceptive portrayal of Melibea, from the point of view of the *carpe diem* philosophy, for they realize that what distinguishes Melibea is not the fact that she falls in love, but that she enjoys while loving. Melibea is the one character whose *carpe diem* transformation can be perceived in its entirety. Celestina's *carpe diem* call transforms Melibea from "doncella," to a woman filled with passion. Rojas' portrayal of Melibea is highly realistic in that we perceive each step of her transformation; for example, she is at first offended by Celestina's allusion to Calisto:

> ¡Ya, ya, ya! Buena vieja, no me digas más, no pases adelante. ¿Ese es el doliente por quién has hecho tantas premisas en tu demanda,... ¡Quemada seas, alcahueta falsa ...(121)

In Act X, however, Melibea finally confesses her lovesickness, in a passage which has been analyzed by some critics as symbolic of sexual penetration or loss of virginity:[76]

> Mi mal es de corazón, la izquierda teta en su aposentamiento, tiende sus rayos
>
> a todas partes. Lo segundo, es nueva-
>
> mente nacido en mi cuerpo, que no pensé
>
> jamás que podía dolor privar el seso,
>
> como éste hace. Túrbame la cara, quítame

---

75 Juan de Valdés 182.

76 See O. Handy 21-24; for a study of the symptoms of lovesickness in the Renaissance see Mary Frances Wack, "The Measure of Pleasure: Peter of Spain on Men, Women, and Lovesickness," *Viator* 17 (1986): 194; Mary Frances Wack, Lovesickness in the Middle Ages: the Viaticum and its commentaries. (Philadelphia: U of Pennsylvania P, 1990.)

el comer, no puedo dormir....(199)

Finally, in Act XIV, we see the final product of the *carpe diem* transformation of Melibea:

> Señor, por Dios, pues ya todo queda por ti,
> pues ya soy tu dueña, pues ya no puedes negar
> mi amor, no me niegues tu vista de día,
> pasando por mi puerta; de noche donde tú
> ordenares. Y más las noches que ordenares,
> sea tu venida por este secreto lugar a la
> misma hora, porque siempre te espere
> apercibida del gozo con que quedo, esperando
> las venideras noches. (24

The servants

If Sempronio follows Celestina's *carpe diem* philosophy, his motives are purely monetary. Potential monetary gain is the motive for Sempronio's seeking Celestina's help in the first place:

> Así es. Calisto arde en amores de Melibea.
> De ti y de mí tiene necesidad. Pues juntos
> nos ha menester, juntos nos aprovechamos;
> que conocer el tiempo y usar el hombre de la
> oportunidad hace los hombres prósperos.
> (71-72)

Throughout, Sempronio is motivated by a desire for "provecho":

> Deseo provecho; querría que este negocio
> hobiese buen fin, no porque saliese mi amo de
> pena, más por salir yo de lacería. (106)

His friendship with Pármeno is also based on monetary interests:

> ¡Oh Pármeno, amigo, cuán alegre y
> provechosa es la conformidad en los
> compañeros! Aunque por otra cosa no nos
> fuera buena Celestina, era harta utilidad
> la que por su causa nos ha venido. (218)

In contrast to Sempronio's monetary motivations, Pármeno's *carpe diem* transformation can be characterized as proceeding from a "wondering sensuality to a

25

state of euphoria and plenitude..."[77] It is the promise made by Celestina of an amorous encounter with Areúsa that convinces him to participate, although Pármeno initially is ". . . the character who has the clearest vision of the transitory quality of life and the inadequacy of living for today":[78]

> A los alegres, serenos y claros soles,
> nublados escuros y lluvias vemos suceder,
> a los solaces y placeres, dolores y muertes
> los ocupan; a las risas y deleites, llantos y
> lloros y pasiones mortales los siguen;
> finalmente, a mucho descanso y sosiego, mucho
> pesar y tristeza. (175)

However, as Pármeno laments the transitory nature of life, he simultaneously eulogizes enjoyment and sexual pleasure:

> ¿Quién podría tan alegre venir como yo
> agora...¿Quién verse, como yo me vi, con
> tanta gloria alcanzada con mi querida
> Areúsa. . . .(175)

Pármeno has learned his *carpe diem* lessons well, as he reiterates the same advice taught to him by Celestina:

> Bien me decía la vieja que de ninguna
> prosperidad es buena la posesión sin
> compañía. El placer no comunicado no es
> placer. (172)

The prostitutes

Even though Areúsa does not appear until the seventh act, we learn about her earlier through the conversations of Celestina and Pármeno. in Act I, and Celestina and Sempronio in Act III. Areúsa is delineated as a spontaneous, natural, and sensual being who pays special attention to the care of her body and thus reveals graphically the *carpe diem* theme. It is Celestina who describes her in the following lines:

> Por hermosa te tenía hasta agora, viendo lo
> que todos podían ver; pero agora te digo que

77 Gilman, *The Art of "La Celestina"* 61.
78 Severin, *Tragicomedy* 84.

no hay en la ciudad tres cuerpos tales como

el tuyo en cuanto yo conozco. No parece que

hayas quince años. (162)

After the deaths of Celestina, Sempronio, and Pármeno, Areúsa too stresses an important principle of the *carpe diem* theme: "Agora nos gozaremos juntas..." (265). Not only does she imitate Celestina in this manner, but she, too, becomes an intermediary figure and "seduces" Sosia in the same way that Celestina influenced Melibea.

In addition to Areúsa, Elicia also plays an important role in communicating the *carpe diem* theme. Despite Elicia's apparently defensive and harsh attitude towards Sempronio, her distinctive ability to teach the *carpe diem* theme can be observed from the very beginning:

No habemos de vivir para siempre. Gocemos

y holguemos, que la vejez pocos la ven...(170)

Elicia repeats the same *carpe diem* theme following the deaths of Celestina, Pármeno, and Sempronio:

Que cuando una puerta se cierra, otra suele

abrir...Con nuevo amor olvidarás losviejos...(256-7)

This passage expresses one aspect in particularof the *carpe diem* theme: the transitory nature of life.

Pleberio

Pleberio adds to the ephemeral note in the *carpe diem* call as he reflects, metaphysically, to Melibea's mother Alisa, on the swift passing of time and the need to marry off their daughter while she is still a young maiden:

Alisa, amiga, el tiempo, según me parece,

se nos va, como dicen, de entre las manos.

Corren los días como agua de río. No hay

cosa tan ligera para huir como la vida (258-259)

The twin themes of virginity, both as a symbol of ripe youth and also, by the potential of its loss, as a portent of the passing of time, are principal elements, as we have seen, of *carpe diem*. The metaphors used by Pleberio, such as "el tiempo que se va entre las manos" and "los días que corren como agua de río," are perhaps what inspired writers of the Baroque such as Quevedo to employ similar imagery, as in the poem "Oh edad mía como te resbalas de entre mis manos."

27

Body Images in Celestina

In order to grasp fully a complete portrayal of the characters in *Celestina* and their expression of the *carpe diem* theme, we must analyze one more essential aspect-- their bodily behavior. Body conduct falls within the realm of extralinguistic behavior. It is a fundamental means of communication. Considered another mode of human behavior, body images deepen characterization.

Before focusing directly on an analysis of body images in *Celestina*, we ought to establish some basic concepts of the body, and the fundamental differences concerning them in medieval and Renaissance philosophies. The concept of the body in the Renaissance differed radically from that of medieval times. The concept of the body can be best understood if perceived within the medieval and Renaissance formulations of the universe and the changes that the latter produced. Indeed, the Renaissance brought about a reconstruction of the artistic and ideological view of the universe that, differed greatly from the medieval view of the cosmos.

> The medieval cosmos, according to Bakhtin, was structured in the following way: The medieval cosmos was built according
>
> to Aristotle. It was based on the precept of the four elements (earth, water, air, and fire), each of which had its rank in the structure of the universe. According to this theory all the elements were subject to a definite order from top to bottom... Celestial bodies, as the most perfect, are endowed with pure movement only, the circular movement around the center of the earth.[79]
>
> In the Renaissance view, the universe was structured differently: The Renaissance destroyed this hierarchical picture of the world; its elements were transferred to one single plane, and the higher and lower stratum became relative. ...This transfer of the world from the vertical to the horizontal was realized in the human body, which became the relative center of the cosmos.[80]

This new awareness of a cosmos in which human beings no longer had to fear their surroundings, but could reign at their center, is reflected in literature. A new emphasis upon material forms permitted Renaissance writers to portray images of

---

79 Bakhtin, *Rabelais* 362-363.
80 Bakhtin, *Rabelais* 363.

what Bakhtin defines as "grotesque realism."[81] The "downward movement" discussed earlier brought with it the lowering of literature "down to the bodily level, especially to the erotic sphere."[82]

This "downward thrust," or shift of focus from the heavens to the material and bodily, can be seen in *Celestina*. The image of the body in *Celestina* is tangible and sensual, and Rojas' constant references to the body are a concrete example of what Bakhtin terms the "lower bodily stratum." The erotic, detailed descriptions of the body in *Celestina* are often exaggerated and at times, as shall be pointed out in chapter II, obscene, underlining this work's approximation to the concept of grotesque realism.

Critics have commented on the subject of the body in Spanish literature, but insufficient emphasis has been placed on the sexual aspect of bodily functions in *Celestina*.[83] Images of sex, as well as food and wine imagery, are an important expression of the *carpe diem* theme as developed by Rojas. These images, which will be discussed in the following section, are frequently used in the *carpe diem* exhortations to seek consolation for life's fragile and transient nature.

In *Celestina*, emphasis is placed on the erotic sensuality and beauty of an exposed, liberated body, which is constantly being glorified. It is what Bakhtin defines as "...the divinization and apotheosis of man."[84] This liberated concept of the body is a reflection of the Renaissance view of the human being as no longer in fear, but rather as occupying the center of the universe and looking down at his/her own body.[85]

Rojas portrays this Renaissance concept of the human being as the center of the universe through his characters. Calisto, for instance, refers to Melibea as his only god, thus divinizing her and her body:

> ¿Quién vido en esta vida cuerpo glorificado de ningún hombre, como agora el mío ...Téngolo por tanto, en verdad, que si Dios me diese en el cielo la silla sobre sus santos, no lo ternía por tanta felicidad. ...¿Yo? Melibeo soy y a Melibea adoro y en Melibea creo y a Melibea amo. (54,59)

---

81 Bakhtin, *Rabelais* 18-19.
82 Bakhtin, *Rabelais* 30-31.
83For a study of the body in Spanish literature see Paul Julian Smith, *The Body Hispanic: Gender and Sexuality in Spanish and Spanish American Literature* (Oxford: Clarendon Press, 1989); Malcolm K. Read, *Visions in Exile: The body in Spanish literature and linguistics: 1500-1800* (Amsterdam/Philadelphia: Purdue U Monographs in Romance Languages, 1989).
84 Bakhtin, *Rabelais* 367.
85 Bakhtin, *Rabelais* 54.

In fact, the body, in *Celestina* , is viewed as a gift from God; its very purpose is that of providing enjoyment. Therefore, bodily expressions of desire, lust and sex, sometimes regarded disparagingly by certain critics, form an integral part of the *carpe diem* theme in *Celestina*. This is why there are constant appraisals and appreciative comments concerning the beauty of the body, as when Pármeno comments on Areúsa's body:

> ...¿qué te contaría de sus gracias de aquella mujer, de su habla y hermosura de cuerpo?...(176)

When the characters recall their moments of pleasure, they do so by referring to their bodies. This is once again a reflection of the new Renaissance philosophy.

Food and Drink in Celestina

Equally important within the *carpe diem* philosophy is the idea of life as a celebration through food and wine. The idea of the feast, or "banquet images," dates back to antiquity:

> Eating and drinking are one of the most significant manifestations of the grotesque body.... The encounter of man with the world, which takes place inside the open, biting, rending, chewing mouth, is one of the most ancient, and most important objects of human thought and imagery.[86]

Wine, comments Bakhtin, "liberates from fear and sanctimoniousness. 'In vino veritas'."[87] This liberating effect of wine is important because it heightens the emphasis upon free expression of sensuality in *Celestina*.

In *Celestina*, eating and drinking, like the body images, are concrete, tangible actions of the body and of the *carpe diem* philosophy.[88] For the characters in *Celestina*, wine and food have several functions.[89] First, wine and food, the symbols of celebration, are an expression of the *carpe diem* philosophy in general-- of pleasure and living the moment, as expressed by Elicia: "Mientra hoy tuviéramos de comer, no pensemos en mañana" (170); and by Celestina: "Goza tu mocedad, el buen día, la buena noche, el buen comer y beber" (154).

Wine, for Celestina, also serves as a consolation for old age and solitude, and as a substitute for the pleasures of youth, as when Celestina comments:

> Poneos en orden, cada uno cabe la suya; yo, que estoy sola, porné cabe mí este jarro y taza, que no es más mi vida de cuanto con ello hablo. Después que me fui haciendo vieja, no sé mejor oficio a la mesa que escanciar... . (184)

Wine and food in *Celestina* are also symbols of friendship, of sharing:

> Juntas comíamos, juntas dormíamos...Si yo traía el pan, ella la carne. Si yo ponía la mesa, ella los manteles...(102-103)

---

86 Bakhtin, *Rabelais* 281; see Pablo A. Cavallero, "Algo más sobre el motivo grecolatino de la vieja bebedora en *Celestina*: Rojas y la tradición de la comediografía," *Celestinesca* 12 (Otoño, 1988): 5-16.
87 Bakhtin, *Rabelais* 286.
88 Gilman, *The Art* 83. He speaks of the Rabelaisian fondness for wine in *Celestina*.
89 Lida, *La Originalidad* 508.

Images of feasting and of eating and drinking in *Celestina*, which occur also in medieval works such as the *Libro de buen amor*, are important, since *Celestina* serves as a model for later works in Spanish literature, in particular for the picaresque novel.[90] Also, through episodes such as the banquet scene in Act IX, we learn about the gastronomical habits of fifteenth-century Spain.[91]

In conclusion, the use of the *carpe diem* theme is not only manifest throughout Celestina, but is also used as a means of persuasion by the protagonist Celestina and the others, thus successfully transforming them into highly sensual characters.

---

90 *Celestina* is considered an important link to the picaresque, as explained by Bruno Mario Damiani, *Francisco Delicado* (New York: Twayne, 1974) 28,40-41,43, 110, 137, 140.
91 See John Lihani, "Spanish Urban Life in the Late Fifteenth Century as Seen in *Celestina*," *Celestinesca* 11 (Otoño, 1987): 21-28.

Chapter   Three

Stylistics and the *carpe diem*

Ever since its publication in 1499, both Renaissance and modern critics have
praised the unique style of *Celestina*. Among Rojas' contemporaries, sixteenth-
century humanist Juan de Valdés eulogizes *Celestina* precisely for its style:

Pacheco.- ... Dezidnos qué os parece del estilo.

Valdés.- El estilo, en la verdad, va bien acomodado a las personas que
hablan...soy de opinión que ningún libro ay escrito en castellano donde
la lengua sté más natural, más propia ni más elegante.[92]

In the description of *Celestina* as   "...bien acomodado a las personas que
hablan..." Valdés summarizes, in one sentence, the very essence of *Celestina's*
unique style. Style in *Celestina* is perceived as a direct extension of the erotic,
sensual world in which the characters are situated.[93] The characters frequently
express themselves in a sensual, erotic tone.

Chapter two of this book explained how the characters utilize the *carpe diem*
philosophy as a way of life and as a means of accomplishing their material and
carnal pursuits. The purpose of Chapter three is to focus on the multiple stylistic
devices that Rojas employs to elicit *carpe diem* . A close analysis of the stylistic traits
in *Celestina* reveals not only the presence of a unique system of *carpe diem*
language and imagery, but also the underlying principle that the *carpe diem* process
is in itself a mode of communication. Given the importance of the *carpe diem* theme
in *Celestina*, the purpose of this study is to analyze the uniqueness of *carpe diem*
imagery, and Rojas' manipulation of the *carpe diem* theme through stylistic devices.
A special idiom of forms and symbols has evolved in *Celestina* which goes far beyond
the traditional *carpe diem* call to enjoyment. The language of the *carpe diem* adds an
innovative dynamism to the theme.

---

92 Juan de Valdés 182.
93 See Rafael Lapesa, *Poetas y prosistas de ayer y de hoy: 20 estudios de historia y crítica
literarias* (Madrid: Gredos, 1977) 63. He comments "Américo Castro habla de la gran influencia
del amor, la importancia del amor en *La Celestina* y su influencia en el estilo."

Before focusing specifically on *carpe diem* language in *Celestina,* it will be pertinent here to stress the general concern that Renaissance writers and philosophers displayed toward the phenomenon of language, and consequently toward the written word. John F. D'Amico describes the humanist preoccupation with language:

> Concern for language, which was at the heart of humanist pedagogy, led to an emphasis on the word as the door to reality.[94]

Indeed, humanists marveled at the powerful forces of language and its infinitely creative capacity. They regarded human speech and the act of communicating as a phenomenon of a miraculous nature. These concepts are expressed by Malcolm K. Read in *The Birth and Death of Language:*

> There are frequent expressions in the Renaissance of a feeling of wonder and awe before the phenomenon of language, more especially before the realization that language, in all its extreme finiteness as a system of signs, can embrace the totality of Man's knowledge of the universe.[95]

While modern scholars tend toward defining language, both spoken and written, as a science, Renaissance scholars, on the other hand, regarded language as a part of a sensory experience:

> Whereas for the modern linguist language is a mere conventional sequence of pho- nemes, for the more 'primitive' mind it is something alive and natural, natural in the sense that there exists an innate, causal relationship between the word and the thing it names.[96]

Despite differences between recent language and linguistic theories as opposed to Renaissance concepts, a general concern for language on the part of both modern and humanist scholars can be observed. This concern for language is linked

---

94 John F. D'Amico, *Theory and Practice in Renaissance Textual Criticism* (Berkeley: U of California P, 1988) 8.

95 Malcolm K. Read, *The Birth and Death of Language: Spanish Literature and Linguistics: 1300-1700* (Madrid: José Porrúa Turanzas, 1983) 70.

96 Malcolm Read, *The Birth* 71. Of the same opinion is Terry Eagleton, *Literary Theory: An Introduction* (Minneapolis: U of Minnesota P, 1983) 38: "Language has also been regarded as a sensory experience: In the early seventeenth century, when the absolute monarchy and the Anglican church still flourished, poets like John Donne and and George Herbert (both conservative Anglicans) displayed a unity of sensibility, an easy fusion of thought and feeling. Language was in direct touch with sensory experience, the intellect was at the tip of the senses, and to have a thought was as physical as smelling a rose."

directly to the idea that language is a social phenomenon in which the being inherently feels the need to communicate.[97]

The Russian semiotician Jurij Lotman defines language precisely as a means of communication:

> ...our concept of language derives from the broad semiotic definition: any ordered system which serves as a means of communication and employs signs...[98]

Based on the principle that language is a form of communication between two or more individuals, the process of communication that occurs in any given system of language involves a sender, a message, and a receiver. As in all art, the literary message is implied in the process of communication.[99]

We can say, therefore, that any given process of communication has its own unique system of language.[100] When Greimas' process of communication is applied to a study of the *carpe diem* in *Celestina*, this produces the following system:

sender=Celestina

message=*carpe diem*

receivers= Calisto, Melibea, Pármeno, Areúsa

1) The sender, Celestina, is the *carpe diem* caller whose task, at the request of Calisto, is to convince Melibea through persuasive arguments to accept her future lover Calisto.

---

97 See Diana Macdonell, *Theories of discourse, An Introduction.* (Oxford, England/New York: Basil Blackwell, 1986) 1-4. Upon defining discourse, Macdonell says that all speech and writng is social. Discourses differ with the kinds of institutions and social practices in which they take shape, and with the positions of those who speak and those whom they address. See also Bakhtin, *The Dialogic* 259 "...verbal discourse is a social phenomenon...."
98 See Jurij Lotman, *The Artistic Structure*, trans. Gail Lenhoff and Ronald Vroon, (Ann Arbor: U of Michigan P, 1977) 6-7.
99 See A.J. Greimas, *Semántica estructural* (Madrid: Gredos, 1971) 203-212; See Lotman 15 "If a work of art communicates something to me, if it serves the goal of communication between sender and receiver, then it is possible to distinguish in the work: 1) a message- that which is transmitted to me; 2) a language- an abstract system, common to sender and receiver, which makes the very act of communication possible.
100 Generative semanticists such as Chafe for example, speak of this system of communication. See Frances Aid, *Semantic Structures in Spanish: A Proposal for Instructional Materials* (Washington D.C.: Georgetown UP, 1973) 2 "...there is a set of universal relational categories at the source of the formation of an utterance that determines the basic organization of the sentence. That is, what one wants to communicate determines the structure of his message."

2) The message is the *carpe diem* call to enjoy youth and carnal pleasures before the inevitable advent of old age and death.

3) The receivers are all the characters who unite: Calisto, Melibea, Pármeno, Areúsa, Sempronio, Elicia.

The speech patterns and imagery used to express the *carpe diem* message result in the creation of a new metalanguage -- that of the *carpe diem*. Mikhail Bahktin refers to communication as a phenomenon consisting of speech systems and speech patterns: "A new type of communication always creates new forms of speech or a new meaning given to the old forms."[101] This model resembles the model of discourse enacted by classical rhetoric, which is

...founded on the necessity of communication: the rhetor takes the object of imitation and attempts to transmit it through the medium of language to the listener....The source of the oration (the speaker), its target (the audience), and the message which passes between them (figurative language) all participate in a single process...[102]

Modern critics have recognized the acute awareness of language in *Celestina*. Malcolm Read comments:

The Renaissance awareness of language is reflected extensively in *Celestina*. It is hard to read the prefatory material of the work without sensing an almost obsessive delight in verbal artifice.[103]

Not only are there metatextual and linguistic concerns in *Celestina*, but also, the art of effective speech and communication is a principle concern in *Celestina*. One of Celestina's main goals is precisely to communicate her *carpe diem* message effectively to others. In the following passage from Act IV, she expresses her concern for communication, as she convincingly persuades Sempronio to follow her plans:

Sempronio, amigo, ni yo me podría parar ni el lugar es aparejado. Vente conmigo delante Calisto, oirás maravillas. Que =será desflorar mi embajada comunicándola con muchos. De mi boca quiero que sepa lo que se ha hecho. (IV;131-132)

Analysis of the system of language in *Celestina*, in which communication is regarded as an essential goal, reveals that the *carpe diem* theme is the common

---

101 Bahktin, *Rabelais* 16.
102 Paul Julian Smith, *Writing in the Margin: Spanish Literature of the Golden Age* (Oxford: Clarendon P, 1988) 44.
103 Malcolm K. Read, *The Birth* 72.

denominator of this system of language. Therefore the *carpe diem* theme plays an essential role in giving *Celestina* a viable textual coherence. As the literary critics Wellek and Warren point out:

> Stylistic analysis seems most profitable to literary study when it can establish some unifying principle, some general aesthetic aim pervasive of a whole work.[104]

The *carpe diem* concept generates a new type of communication consisting of its own structure of multiple signs, verbs, metaphors, and vocabulary which can be systematically analyzed in *Celestina*.

It was stated previously that the stylistic traits in *Celestina* reflect the erotic, sensual world of the characters in the novel. This is achieved precisely through speech and language. It is by means of speech, affirms Read, that the characters and subsequently the reader of *Celestina* are introduced into the erotic world of the novel. Our task here is to discover the general code of the *carpe diem*-- to decipher the signs of *carpe diem* expression. It will be shown how a direct link exists between the word and sex: "However, though erotic exchange ('intercourse') is in essence closely interwoven with linguistic interaction ('discourse'), in *Celestina* sexuality competes with language with abnormal tenacity:..."[105]

The unique sensuality of the language in *Celestina* has been analyzed by numerous critics.[106] While these studies have provided an interesting analysis of language in *Celestina*, the present chapter explores in greater detail the entire system of *carpe diem* language. The following aspects of the *carpe diem* system of language and imagery are to be discussed:

1. The *carpe diem* system of verbs
2. *Carpe diem* language and imagery
3. Nonverbal *carpe diem* imagery
4. Laughter and comical imagery

---

104 René Wellek and Austin Warren, *Theory of Literature*, 3rd ed. (San Diego/New York: Harcourt Brace Jovanovich, 1942) 182.
105 Read, *The Birth* 74
106 See Read, *The Birth*; Boullosa, *La idea*.

1. The *carpe diem* system of verbs

Celestina is replete with discussions on the need to enjoy youth and carnal pleasures. Throughout the novel, the terminology that Celestina employs in her *carpe diem* exhortations is made up of images that graphically evoke the theme of enjoyment and pleasure. For example, one of the ways in which the theme "seize the day" is projected is by the frequent use of verbs of enjoyment. These and other verbal expressions will therefore be examined in detail in both their semantic and temporal aspects.

Linguists have viewed the verb as being a central component of the semantic structure of a sentence.[107] Verbs and the semantic patterns that they form, play an important role in the expression of the *carpe diem* theme in *Celestina*, and verbs are a principal means of setting the mood of this theme.

Carpe diem verbs of enjoyment

This first category of verbs consists of all verbs in *Celestina* that express the fundamental principle of the *carpe diem* concept, the call to enjoy life. These verbs and their derivative nominalized forms occur frequently in *Celestina*.[108] The following are classified as verbs of enjoyment and are used by almost all the characters: "gozar," "deleitar," "amar," "gustar," "holgar," "besar," "morder," "tocar," "dormir," "vivir," "allegar," "ver."

The most frequently used verb of this category is "gozar." A prototype *carpe diem* verb, it sets the tone of intimacy and eroticism in *Celestina*, symbolizing both carnal pleasure and overall enjoyment and happiness.

In Act I, Calisto utilizes the verb "gozar" and the noun "deleite" to both express and conceal his love and sexual desire for Melibea. Even though "gozar" and "deleitar" are used ironically to parody religion, the erotic connotations of "deleite" can be observed:

---

107 See Frances Aid, *Semantic* 6, where she discusses the verb and its function within the case study. Cases are "...propositional, having an intimate relation with the verb such that their typical presence can be said to be a criterion for classifying lexical sets among verbs of a language."; See Juan Martínez Marín, *Sintaxis de la Celestina: La oración compuesta.* (Granada: Colección filológica de la Universidad de Granada) 295.

108 See Juan Martinez Marin, *Sintaxis* 149-158 for an extensive study of verbs which includes "gozar" and prepositions that accompany the verb.

¿Quien vido en esta vida cuerpo glorificado de ningun hombre, como agora el mío? Por cierto, los gloriosos santos, que se deleitan, no gozan más que yo agora en el acatamiento tuyo. (I;54)

Later, in Act VI, Calisto exclaims while waiting impatiently for Melibea's "cordón":

> Y mándame mostrar aquel santo cordón, que tales miembros fue digno de ceñir. ¡Gozarán mis ojos con todos los otros sentidos, pues juntos han sido apasionados! ¡Gozará mi lastimado corazón, aquel que nunca recibió momento de placer después que aquella señora conoció! Todos los sentidos le llagaron, todos acorrieron a él con sus esportillas de trabajo. Cada uno le lastimó cuanto más pudo; los ojos en vella, los oídos en oilla, las manos en tocalla. (VI;144-5)

Here the verb "gozar" has kinesthetic connotations because enjoyment encompasses sight and touch: "gozarán mis ojos, gozará mi lastimado corazón."

Upon Calisto's erotic encounter with Melibea, he exclaims:

> Mora en mi persona tanta turbación de placer, que me hace no sentir todo el gozo que poseo. (XIV;242)

When he caresses Melibea he uses the verb "gozar" to express sexual pleasure:

> Perdona, señora, a mis desvergonzadas manos, que jamás pensaron de tocar tu ropa con su indignidad y poco merecer; agora gozan de llegar a tu gentil cuerpo y lindas y delicadas carnes. (XIV;243)

The use of verbs of enjoyment is one of Celestina's main techniques of *carpe diem* persuasion; verbs make her speeches highly effective and convincing:

> Gocémonos y aprovechémonos, que sobre el partir nunca reñiremos. (V;132)

Celestina uses "gozar" to persuade Melibea to see Calisto:

> Señora, el perdón sobraría done el yerro falta. De Dios seas perdonada, que buena compañía me queda. Dios la deje gozar su noble juventud y florida mocedad, que es el tiempo en que más placeres y mayores deleites se alcanzarán...(IV;115)

Celestina systematically uses the verb "gozar" to convince and reinforce her *carpe diem* philosophy:

> Goza tu mocedad, el buen día, la buena noche, el buen comer y beber. (VII;154)

This verb is constantly repeated as in the following passage in Act VII in which Celestina appraises Areúsa's body.

¡Oh quién fuera hombre y tanta parte alcanzara de ti para gozar tal
vista!... Y pues tú no puedes de ti propia gozar, goce quien puede.
(VII;162)

It is through the use of verbs of enjoyment that Celestina's speeches
themselves are transformed into acts of enjoyment. These verbs become mirror
images of the characters' pleasure in enjoyment. Celestina, for example, enjoys
watching others in the act of enjoyment and talking about it:

El deleite es con los amigos en las cosas sensuales y especial en recontar
las cosas de amores y comunicarlas: "Esto hice, esto otro me dijo, tal
donaire pasamos, de tal manera la tomé, así la besé...(I;88)

Through the verb "gozar," Celestina implies that she has experienced sexual
love, as she recalls her youth:

Parece, hija, que no sé yo qué cosa es esto, que nunca vi estar un
hombre con una mujer juntos y que jamás pasé por ello no gocé de lo
que gozas y que no sé lo que pasan y lo que dicen y hacen. (VII;168)

Derivatives of the verb "gozar" include not only nouns such as "gozo" and
"deleite," but also related nouns and adjectives that accompany "gozar," such as
"joven," and "mancebo."

Those who continue preaching the *carpe diem* theme use the same verbs to
express the *carpe diem*, as can be observed in the following lines spoken by Elicia:

No habemos de vivir para siempre. Gocémonos y holguemos, que la vejez
pocos la ven.... (VII;170)

Melibea also expresses her desire to enjoy Calisto's love, as she pleads with her
servant Lucrecia to be discreet about her secret love affair:

Ruégote, por Dios, se cubra con secreto sello, porque yo goce de tan
suave amor. (X;206)

A chain reaction occurs when the verb "gozar" is used. "Gozar" is a quasi-
magical verb; it is a means of justification for the actions of Melibea and the others.
It enables Melibea to enjoy Calisto, and her parents to enjoy her; it lets Melibea enjoy
her youth, and subsequently her parents can enjoy their old age:

Déjenme mis padres gozar de él, si ellos quieren gozar de mí. No piensen
en estas vanidades ni en estos casamientos; que más vale ser buena
amiga que mala casada. Déjenme gozar mi mocedad alegre, si quieren
gozar su vejez cansada....(XVII;261)

Regretting the loss of her lover, Melibea once again uses the verb "gozar" and
its corresponding nominalization, "¿Cómo no gocé más del gozo?" (IXX;285), to express

40

her regret at not having enjoyed enough. She also uses the verb "gozar" as a justification of her acts when she confesses her affair to her father in Act XX:

> ...yo fui causa que la tierra goce sin tiempo el más noble cuerpo y más fresca juventud ... Perdí mi virginidad; del cual deleitoso yerro de amor gozamos casi un mes.(XX;291)

Note the symmetry of one of the final uses of "gozo," in the last act of *Celestina*, when Pleberio, after witnessing Melibea's suicide, says: "nuestro gozo en el pozo"(XI;293). Like the *carpe diem* theme itself, which ends in destruction, here Rojas discards the image of enjoyment as "gozo" is destroyed.

Communication verbs

In addition to verbs of enjoyment, verbs of communication and sharing also form an important part of the *carpe diem* system of language and imagery.

Throughout the centuries, philosophers and writers have commented extensiveley on the human need to communicate. Aristotle claimed that the human being is by nature a social animal and therefore has an inherent need to communicate. Taking this principle one step further, Bakhtin claims that it is through others that the individual acquires his or her identity:

> Todo lo que a mi concierne, llega a mi conciencia, comenzando por mi nombre, desde el mundo exterior a través de la palabra de los otros....Yo me conozco inicialmente a través de otros....[109]

When the Russian writer Dostoevsky comments, "ser significa comunicarse," he too alludes to the concept of communication as a necessary part of being and existing.[110]

In *Celestina* the verbs "recontar," "comunicar," "aprovechar," "hablar," "dar," and "compartir," all express the act of communicating and sharing. Communicating one's thoughts and previous actions is as important as performing the sex act. In fact, the word itself becomes a form of pleasure, because part of the pleasure of sex is derived from the pleasure of speaking and communicating about it to others. Textually, communicating one's pleasures is equally as important as the sex act itself, as illustrated in the following passage:

> El deleite es con los amigos en las cosas sensuales y especial en recontar las cosas de amores y comunicarlas: "esto hice, esto otro me dijo, tal donaire pasamos, de tal manera la tomé, así la besé, así me mordió, así la abracé, así se allegó. ¡Oh qué habla! ¡Oh qué gracia! ¡Oh qué juegos! ¡Oh qué besos! Vamos allá, volvamos acá, ande la música, pintemos los motes, cantemos canciones, invenciones, justemos...." (I;88)

Like enjoyment, communication and sharing are important parts of the *carpe diem* philosophy. In *Celestina*, sharing has, of course, ironic implications. As Mendeloff points out, in *Celestina*, behind the humanitarian concept of sharing lies a selfish, monetary motive on the part of Celestina and the servants. In any event, it is through verbs of communication and sharing that Celestina persuades the others to follow her exhortations:

---

109 Mikhail Bakhtin, *Estética de la creación verbal* (México: Siglo veintiuno editores, S.A., 1982) 360.
110 Bakhtin, *Estética* 360.

Ganemos todos, partamos todos, holguemos todos. (I;79)

In addition, the idea of sharing has erotic overtones, as expressed in the proverb:

...que los bienes, si no son comunicados, no son bienes. (I;79)

Within the *carpe diem* concept is the idea that it is a sin not to share the body and its pleasures:

> Por Dios, pecado ganas en no dar parte de estas gracias a todos los que bien te quieren. Que no te las dio Dios para que pasasen en balde por la frescor de tu juventud. ...(VII;162)

In another scene, to fully enjoy pleasure, Pármeno must verbalize the night he spent with Areúsa to Sempronio:

> ¿a quién contaría yo este gozo? (VII;172) Pues que es todo el placer que traigo si no haberla alcanzado...(VII;173)

Verbs signalling death and dying

Diametrically opposed to verbs of enjoyment and communication are verbs that express the grim side of the *carpe diem* motif. Verbs such as "morir" and "envejecer," "descender," "secar," and "entristecer" express the inevitable fate of human beings, who, in spite of efforts to control life, are ".....nacidos para morir...." (IV;120).[111] Although these verbs are used less frequently than the verbs of enjoyment and communication, Celestina does employ them as part of her *carpe diem* philosophy. They add a more profound, philosophical tone to her speeches and dramatize even further the need to enjoy youth, as they add a tone of finality to the *carpe diem* theme:

> Desean harto mal para sí, desean harto trabajo. Desean llegar allá, porque porque llegando viven y el vivir es dulce y viviendo envejecen. (IV;115)
>
> Pero bien sé que subí para descender, florecí para secarme, gocé para en- tristecerme, nací para vivir, viví para crecer, crecí para envejecer, envejecí para morirme. (IX;193)

Through the use of antitheses[112] or binary oppositions, or opposing images such as subir/descender, florecer/secar, gozar/entristecer, nacer/vivir, vivir/crecer, envejecer/morir, the more somber side of the carpe diem theme is expressed to its fullest. These binary oppositions, as we shall see later on, have highly sexual connotations and do not have the normal imprisoning effect that they conventionally do in *carpe diem* poetry, for instance-- a point which is discussed in Chapter four. The above oppositions, however, delineate the cyclical nature of the *carpe diem* and the fact that the human being, like all other creatures, is born to die.

An analysis of *carpe diem* verbs in *Celestina* also reveals the importance of imperative forms. The above-mentioned verbs, and verbs of enjoyment in particular, are often in the imperative form. It is through the use of the imperative form that the *carpe diem* acquires its authoritative tone.[113] The use of the command forms

---

111 See Severin, *Tragicomedy* 83-90.
112 On antitheses see Charles F. Fraker, "Declamation and the Celestina," *Celestinesca* 9 (1985): 47-62.
113 Berrio 249, defines the imperative in *carpe diem* poetry as "imperativos semánticos"; On authoritative speech see Bakhtin, *Dialogic.*; D.J. Gifford, "Magical Patter: The Place of Verbal Fascination in La Celestina," *Medieval and Renaissance Studies on Spain and Portugal in Honour of*

"goza," "gozad," "gocémonos," "aprovechémonos," informs the characters and the reader of *Celestina* of the urgency not to waste valuable time, and to heed the *carpe diem* call. The following passage from Act V exemplifies the typical authoritative tone created by the imperative mode:

> Gocémonos y aprovechémonos, que sobre el partir n u n c a reñiremos...(V;132)

The use of the first person plural imperative is particularly effective because it includes both characters and reader in the command and therefore anticipates and encourages participation. Inherent in the imperative form is the constant use of the present tense, which "...eliminates everything that is non-essential to the situation of the speakers."[114]

The previous classifications of verbs dealt with the *carpe diem* from a semantic perspective. This part of Chapter three analyzes diverse motifs and various types of expressions involving time, as well as imagery.

The human being's preoccupation with chronological time and its symbolic representation has been a recurrent theme in Spanish literature from the medieval writer Jorge Manrique and his poem "Coplas que hizo por la muerte de su padre," to the Baroque lyric poetry of Góngora and Quevedo. In *carpe diem* poetry, images of the clock and other mechanical instruments such as the hour glass and sun dial all communicate to the reader the desperate anguish of time's irreversible passing. Renaissance humanist Luis Vives considered time and the human awareness of time to be precisely what distinguishes humans from other animals:

> The human characteristics which Vives singles out for attention. Man's lack of instinctive behavior; his knowledge of past and future time, his awareness of death, his possession of a private inner world, the freedom of his will, his singular restlessness-- are those of a creature who has raised himself above the natural world.[115]

In the Introduction, it was stated that the *carpe diem* concept is inherently paradoxical. The human preoccupation with the irreversible passing of time on the

---

P.E. Russell, ed. F.W. Hodcroft, D.G. Pattison, R.D.F. Pring-Mill, R.W. Truman, (Oxford: The Society for the Studies of Medieval Languages and Literature, 1981) 30, speaks of deliberate style and choice of words in *La Celestina*, and that incantation is a stylistic device that gives an authoritative tone because of hypnotic effect.

114 Severin, *Memory*, footnote 32.

115 Read, *Birth* 54.

one hand, is in contradiction with the inevitability of human mortality. Like the *carpe diem* theme itself, the concept of time is paradoxical.[116]

As we recall, the *carpe diem* call to enjoy life is precisely an attempt to control the irreversible flight of time. Within the scope of the *carpe diem* theme, time is conceived of as an endless deferring of the present. In *Celestina*, there is constant concern with the linear sequence of events and a deliberate effort on the part of the characters to control time either by stopping the clock: ". . .ten tú el tiempo que no ande; terné yo mi forma, que no se mude." (IV;118); or by speeding chronological time in order to achieve full pleasure:

> ¡Oh luciente Febo, date priesa a tu acostumbrado camino! ¡Oh deleitosas estrellas, apareceos ante de la cotinua orden! (XIV;249) [117]

Critics have also commented on certain inconsistencies concerning the relation between time and space in *Celestina*. Humanist critic Juan de Valdés criticized the brevity of time involved in bringing about the downfall of Melibea. Asensio claims there is an "antinomía entre el tiempo y la acción." Bonilla y San Martín criticize the rapid transition of Melibea from a state of anger to a state of desire.

If we accept the Bakhtinian concept of "time= space" or the chronotope, not only are there no longer inconsistencies in *Celestina* such as the ones mentioned above by critics, but also, these apparent inconsistencies are deliberate in the novel and show once again the paradoxical nature of time and its inevitable forces. It seems that the inconsistencies in time and space in *Celestina* are deliberate in an attempt to express the paradox of time as an endless deferring of the present.[118]

---

116 Daniel L. Heiple, *Mechanical Imagery in Spanish Golden Age Poetry* (Madrid: José Porrúa Turanzas, 1983) 110 "...the idea of capturing an ideal moment or of existing in an unchanging immovable eternity is in direct contradiction to the many passing moments that confront man in the earthly progression of time. Man senses and reacts emotionally to the irreversible progression of events that he cannot change and which signify his own personal destruction. Existence as a progression of time and decay has always perturbed mankind, who has found consolation in various concepts of static, never–decaying existence. The problem of the mutability of the world and time is an old question, found in the earliest of literature such as the *Lamentations of Jeremiah* and the pre-Socratic philosophers, especially Heraclitus and Zeno of Elea, who propounded logical paradoxes on the contradictions of permanence and flux."

117 See Berndt 92 "Desde el comienzo de la obra, notamos una agudísima conciencia del paso del tiempo por parte de los personajes. Todos tienen presente el hecho de que la vida humana está limitada por la muerte."; Severin, *Memory* 2; Lida, *Dos Obras* 85-88.

118 Bakhtin, *Dialogic* 84 "We shall give the name 'chronotope' (literally "time space") to the intrinsic connectedness of temporal and spatial relationships that are artistically expressed in literature. This term [space-time] is employed in mathematics, and was introduced as part of Einstein's Theory of Relativity...What counts for us is the fact that it expresses the inseparability of space and time (time as the fourth dimension of space)..."

The critic and reader of *Celestina* should not attempt a linear reconstruction of the events and the chronology of *Celestina*, but should focus rather on the constant awareness of time, and the characters' attempt to beat the clock. Given the notion of the chronotope, inconsistencies such as the ones pointed out by Severin and others no longer exist.

The concept of time itself can be viewed as a delusion and an anachronism. The inconsistencies in *Celestina* concerning time approximate those of philosophers who conceptualized time as a phenomenon which can be divided into two different notions:

> All of the Renaissance and Baroque conflicts of time can be viewed as manifestations of the basic dichotomy of the mental conception of static time as opposed to the experience of fluid ever-moving time.[119]

In *Celestina* as in the *carpe diem* concept, a dichotomy exists between chronological time and psychological time. One of the ways in which the *carpe diem* theme manifests itself, is through the characters constant awareness of time.

Time indicators manifest themselves in two distinct forms in *Celestina*. Firstly, they are found in the form of philosophical discussions or monologues on the notion of time and the brevity of life. Celestina, for example, warns youth not to let biological time go by without fully enjoying youth:

> Gozad vuestras frescas mocedades, que quien tiempo tiene y mejor le espera, tiempo viene que se arrepiente; como yo hago agora por algunas horas que dejé perder, cuando moza, cuando me preciaba, cuando me querían. (IX;189-190)

The philosophical expression of time is graphically expressed by Calisto in his monologue:

> ¡Oh espacioso reloj, aun te vea yo arder en vivo fuego de amor! Que si tú esperases lo que yo, cuando des doce, jamás estarías arrendado a tu voluntad del maestro que te compuso. Pues, ¡vosotros, invernales meses, que agora estáis escondidos, viniesedes con vuestras muy cum- plidas noches a torcarlas por estos prolijos días! Ya me parece haber un año que no he visto aquel suave descanso, aquel deleitoso refrigerio de mis trabajos. ¿Pero qué es lo que demando? ¿Qué pido, loco, sin sufrimiento? Lo que jamás fue ni puede ser. No aprenden los cursos naturales a rodearse sin orden, que a todos es un igual curso, a todos un mismo

119 Heiple 125.

espacio para muerte y vida, un limitado término a los secretos
movimientos del alto firmamento celestial de los planetas, y norte de los
crecimientos y mengua de la menstrua luna. Todo se rige con un freno
igual, todo se mueve con igual espuela: cielo, tierra, mar, fuego, viento,
calor, frío. ¿Qué me aprovecha a mí me dé doce horas el reloj de hierro,
si no las ha dado el del cielo? Pues, por mucho que madrugue, no
amanece más aína. Pero tú, dulce imaginación, tú que puedes, me acorre.
(XIV;249-250)

Because of his longing for Melibea, and through his imagination and memory,
Calisto evokes *carpe diem* images. The image of the clock triggers an entire
philosophical monologue which focuses on his own transcendence. Calisto has
created interesting mirror images, for as he looks at the clock he sees himself-- he
has created an illusion (time) through another illusion, his memories of a love scene.
The juxtaposition of the clock and his memories of passion delineates, through
various cinematographic techniques such as "montage," flashbacks, and the shot
reverse shot, images, of the "reloj" and "vivo fuego de amor."[120] He therefore
graphically expresses the contradiction that exists between the inevitable
chronological order of time symbolized in the "relox de hierro," and his passion,
which implies his desire to stop time. He even distinguishes between fabricated
human time in the form of instruments such as the "relox de hierro," and cosmic
time, "el del cielo," as he cynically and pessimistically concludes: "¿Qué me aprovecha
a mí me dé doce horas el reloj de hierro, si no las ha dado el del cielo?" He even goes so
far as to personify the clock as he turns an inanimate object into an animate one by
addressing the clock as if it were a person: "Que si tú esperases lo que yo, cuando des
doce, jamás estarías arrendado a tu voluntad del maestro que te compuso." He offers
the clock a hypothetical situation and through his projecting concludes that the
clock, too, if human, would rebel, just like himself, against the chronological order of
time. He has created a fourth temporal dimension-- one that oscillates between the
past and future, one that is simultaneously temporal and spatial.

The second form of time indicators includes the shorter references that all the
characters make either to the hour, the need to hurry, or the time of day (morning,
evening). Even though at first glance these short time indicators can perhaps be
perceived as trivial in comparison with the longer, more dramatic and somber
monologues, comments such as "no dejemos pasar el tiempo en balde," "es tarde," "no

---

120 For an analysis of cinematographic techniques see André Bazin, *What is Cinema?*, trans.
Hugh Gray ((Berkeley: U of California P, 1967.)

tardemos," "se va haciendo noche," "¿amanece ya?" are all indicators of time awareness.

2. *Carpe diem* language and imagery

Celestinesque language has often been the subject of diverse criticism.[121] Even the theatrical and cinematographical representations of *Celestina* have incited controversial critical reviews, concerning certain linguistic and bodily obscenities.[122] The low language of *Celestina* is a direct reflection of the tendency of the novel to depict the low world. The language and imagery of *Celestina* create a free, sensual, erotic atmosphere which can be defined according to the Bakhtinian concept of "images of the material bodily lower stratum."[123]

The basic principle set forth by Bakhtin in his study of Rabelais can also be applied to *Celestina*. Bakhtin states that popular culture and the concept of the carnival of the "world inside out" influenced literature in that it introduced a new system of images and speech patterns reflective of the "low world"-- that is, abusive, profane, and indecent language. This trend, which in literary expression takes the form of grotesque realism, is characteristic in some literature of the Renaissance.[124] Bakhtin tells us that the basic principal of grotesque realism is degradation; that is, a shift in sphere from high to low. The language of the lower bodily stratum gives way to an entire system of imagery that is oriented towards the "genital zone."

Language and imagery in *Celestina* form part of the same system that Bakhtin defines as the lower bodily stratum. This language of degradation is deliberate in *Celestina*; Rojas has purposely chosen degrading vocabulary, language, and imagery to create the free, sensual, erotic atmosphere that is needed in order to convince characters to "seize the day."[125] Rojas has therefore repudiated the "high" or conventional vocabulary and the traditional Petrarchan images of angelic hair, rosy

---

121See Read, *Birth* 72.

122 See Michelle S. de Cruz-Saenz "Representación de la Tragicomedia de Calisto y Melibea: Compañía Teatro del Aire (Madrid), En una gira por los EE.UU." *Celestinesca* 6 (Mayo, 1982): 35-37. In her review of the theatrical presentation of the above-mentioned group, she refers to 37 frequent images showing nudity and sexually-oriented scenes.

123 Bakhtin, *Rabelais.*

124 For a study of Renaissance erotica, see David O. Frantz, *Festum Voluptatis* (Columbus: Ohio State UP, 1989) 10. Frantz claims that use of vulgar words and sexual metaphors was common in the Renaissance.

125 Gifford 30, speaks of style as being deliberate in use of language and choice of words.

cheeks, and coral lips; he opts instead for the lower bodily stratum vocabulary of whores, bawds, sex, and dirty jokes.

The deliberate use of metaphors in a given text is linked with the speaker's intentions.[126] The speakers in *Celestina* communicate lower bodily stratum discourse explicitly, through their use of language and metaphors which include semantically sexual. meanings.

Before we continue our study of *carpe diem* language and imagery in *Celestina*, let us define two basic terms necessary for this study: metaphor and imagery. Metaphor can be defined as being semantically oriented.[127] Rojas' use of metaphors adds thematic cohesiveness to the *carpe diem* motif. A broad definition of the term imagery, applicable to this study, is "any concrete representation of a sense impression."[128]

The *carpe diem* language of *Celestina* often includes "catachresis"[129] in which metaphors create a free, erotic, atmosphere; they are catalysts of the truly liberating process that occurs in the novel; they reflect the power of imagination inherent in *Celestina*. As Allen Deyermond notes: "The interplay of metaphors and reality contributes notably to *Celestina's* imaginative power."[130]

Exemplary of this shift in spheres from "high" language (courtly tradition) to "low" language (grotesque realism) are the descriptions of Melibea given by Calisto in Act I and later by Areúsa in Act IX. Calisto's description is representative of the Renaissance concept of beauty:

> Los ojos verdes, rasgados; las pestañas luengas; las cejas delgadas y alzadas... los labrios colorados...el pecho alto; la redondeza y forma de las pequeñas tetas...(I;66)

---

126 See Max Black "Metaphor" from *Philosophical Perspectives on Metaphor*, ed. Mark Johnson (Minneapolis: U of Minnesota P, 1981) 67 "There are indefinitely many contexts (including nearly all the interesting ones) where the meaning of a metaphorical expression has to be reconstructed from the speaker's intentions (and other clues) because the broad rules of standard usage are too general to supply the information needed."
127 Max Black 63-82 "So to call a sentence an instance of metaphor is to say something about its meaning, not about i[t]s orthography, its phonetic pattern, or its grammatical form. (To use a well-known distinction, "metaphor" must be classified as a term belonging to "semantics" and not to "syntax" - to any physical inquiry about language.")
128 Heiple 18.
129 Max Black 69 "So viewed, metaphor is a species of 'catachresis', which I shall define as the use of a word in some new sense in order to remedy a gap in the vocabulary."
130 Alan D. Deyermond, "Hilado-Cordón-Cadena: Symbolic Equivalences in *La Celestina*" *Celestinesca* 1 (Mayo, 1977): 6-12.

Although Calisto's description of Melibea is graphic, the transformation of language that occurs in Areúsa's description exemplifies a much more vulgar, exaggerated form of imagery:

> Que así goce de mí, unas tetas tiene, para ser doncella, como si tres veces hobiese parido; no parecen sino dos grandes calabazas. El vientre no se le he visto; pero juzgando por lo otro, creo que le tiene tan flojo como vieja de cincuenta años...(IX;186)

The image "pequeñas tetas" is thus transformed into "grandes calabazas." This shift in vocabulary is the result of what Bakhtin defines as the downward thrust of images. In *Rabelais and His World*, Bakhtin describes this evolution in vocabulary as a reflection of the conceptual reconstruction of the medieval topography of the universe from vertical to the new Renaissance cosmos which is horizontal. A shift from a vertical spatial orientation to a horizontal produces new imagery that focuses on the human being and on the body. This change from top to bottom occurs both in space and metaphor and as a result, produces both a rejuvenation of the biological individual,and an abundance of erotic images. This shift can be observed in Calisto's description of Melibea, after his first encounter with her in Act XIV, which changes from "¡Oh angélica imagen; o preciosa perla ante quien el mundo es feo; o mi señora y mi gloria!" to "...en mis brazos te tengo y no lo creo."(XIV;242)

Exemplary of sexually oriented language is the use of "llegar" and "alcanzar" to signify achievement of the sex act. Celestina jokingly says to Pármeno:

> Llégate acá, putico, que no sabes nada del mundo ni de sus deleites. ¡Más rabia mala me mate, si te llego a mí, aunque vieja! (I;82)

Note the shift in meaning of "llegar," from its meaning of location to its sexual meaning: "llégate" becomes "te llego a mí". Celestina frequently use the verb "llegar" in a sexual way: "Allégate a mí, ven acá, que mil azotes y puñadas te di en este mundo y otros tantos besos."(I;84) In the scene praising Areúsa's body, Celestina uses "alcanzar" meaning to reach sexually: "¡Oh quién fuera hombre y tanta parte alcanzara de ti para gozar tal vista!" (VII;162). An explicit definition of "alcanzar" is given by Pármeno when he refers not only to the sex act but to the possibility of pregnancy:[131]

> Sempronio: ¡A qué llamas haberla alcanzado? ¿Estaba a alguna ventana o qué es eso? Pármeno: A ponerla en duda si queda preñada o no. (VIII;175)

---

[131] The definition of the bodily lower stratum, as defined by Bakhtin, includes reproduction and pregnancy.

Words conventionally classified as pertaining to the high sphere shift to the lower sphere. The word "gloria" no longer means religious ecstasy but rather sexual ecstasy. After his encounter with Areúsa, when Pármeno asks: "¿A quién daré parte de mi gloria?" (VII;172), he refers to the glory of the pleasure of sex. Like "gozo," "gloria," too, means sexual satisfaction. This idea is expressed by Calisto: "Bien me huelgo que estén semejantes testigos [manos] de mi gloria" (XIV;243)[132]. The basic lexicon of *Celestina* can be classified also as part of the lower bodily stratum. Words such as "puta," "puto," "puta vieja," "necia," "tetas," "la madre," and "pechos," are all characteristic of the sexual sphere. These words, which are used repeatedly in *Celestina*, all refer either directly or indirectly to genital zones.

Language is so suggestive in *Celestina* that sexual discourse becomes a kind of textuality:

> Trae a mi fantasía la presencia angélica de aquella imagen luciente; vuelve a mis oídos el suave son de sus palabras, quellos desvíos sin gana, aquel «Apártate allá, señor, no llegues a mí»; aquel «No seas descortés», que con sus rubicundos labrios veía sonar; aquel «No quieras mi perdición», que de rato en rato proponía; aquellos amorosos abrazos entre palabra y palabra, aquel soltarme y prenderme, aquel huir y llegarse, aquellos azucarados besos...(XIV;250)

Another example of the shift that occurs from top to bottom in the *carpe diem* imagery of *Celestina* is the use of binary oppositions, which are discussed further in Chapter four. These opposing images are traditionally used within the *carpe diem* context to accentuate the paradoxical nature of life and the opposing forces of youth and enjoyment versus old age and death.[133] In *Celestina*, however, binary oppositions such as subir/descender, florecer/secar, love as amarga/dulce, go far beyond the traditional realm of the *carpe diem* in that they are symbolic of positive sex forces on the one hand, and negative sex forces on the other.[134] They are much stronger then mere "oxímoros."[135] This is yet another instance of what Black refers

---

132 See Dorothy Sherman Severin, ed., *La Celestina*, by Fernando de Rojas (Madrid: Cátedra, 1987) 285; footnote 8: "Gloria parece ser usado como eufemismo sexual, al igual que gozo..."
133 Gilhead 133.
134 The concept of oppositions can be compared to the theory of vertical spatial concepts found in Chapter 8 titled "The Composition of the Verbal Work of Art" from Jurij Lotman's *The Structure of the Artistic Space.* 218. According to Lotman this creates a model of a vertically oriented universal system.
135 Lapesa 63, "Así cobra sentido la abundancia de oxímoros como los que emplea Celestina para definir el amor."

to as "catachresis." Metaphors here are metatextual; that is, they are signs that take on new signifiers. This is what gives *Celestina* its dialectical nature.

Celestina's definition of "amor dulce" in Act X illustrates these opposing negative and positive sexual forces:

> Es un fuego escondido, una agradable llaga, un sabroso veneno, una dulce amargura, unadelectable dolencia, un alegre tormento, una dulce y fiera herida, una blanda muerte. (X;203)

Upon hearing Calisto's name, as if in allusion to the sexual connotations of "blanda muerte," Melibea faints. Through paradox and antithesis, Rojas thus succeeds in employing the classical *carpe diem* to portray a highly erotic way of life where sexuality has replaced textuality.

3. Non Verbal Imagery

The representation of the body, and bodily discourse, form an essential part of the *carpe diem* system of imagery. In *Celestina*, Rojas exceeds the conventional paradigm of the *carpe diem* through his use of body language.[136] Equally as effective as verbal imagery, nonverbal imagery has been perceived as being the highest form of understanding:

> No wonder that for many cultures the highest form of understanding is something beyond words and is associated with non verbal forms of communication: music, love, the emotional language of paralinguistics.[137]

It was stated previously that in *Celestina*, "...sexuality competes with language with abnormal tenacity..."[138] to the point where sexuality replaces textuality.[139] Sexuality is expressed through the body and its functions(vision, speech, hearing, gestures, laughter, crying, drinking, eating, and copulation). The body and bodily functions acquire so much autonomy in *Celestina* that these bodily functions, sex in particular, generate a separate form of discourse. The body, therefore, can be viewed as a "social signifier":

> From an empirical viewpoint, the body is a concrete, observable object, but, viewed within a sign system, the body is a social signifier...[140]

Sexuality is a form of discourse in *Celestina*.[141] Just as *carpe diem* language and imagery in *Celestina* are characterized as pertaining to the bodily lower stratum, descriptions of the body, along with body language and bodily functions, reveal the

---

136 See Paul Julian Smith, *Quevedo on Parnassus: Allusion and Theory in the Love-lyric* (London: Modern Humanities Research Association, 1987) 59. What distinguishes *La Celestina* from typical "carpe diem" poetry as far as body images are concerned, is that the graphic visualization of the body is not that of images of "future deformity" but those of rejuvenating, vital images of the body.

137 Lotman, *Artistic* 56.

138 Read, *Birth* 74.

139 Read 74

140 Nelly Furman, "The Politics of Language: beyond the gender principle?," *Making a Difference. Feminist Literary Criticism*, ed. Gayle Green, Coppélia Kahn (New York: Routledge, 1985) 73.

141 Diana Macdonell 1-4. Says that discourse can be verbal or nonverbal. Non-verbal discourse deals with the interchange of signs. Whatever signifies or has meaning can be considered part of discourse. It is also convenient here to recall Lotman's open definition of language as being: "Every system whose end is to establish communication between two or more individuals may be defined as language." *Structure* 7.

54

very same shift in spheres. The main preoccupation of the characters is how to derive pleasure from the bodily functions and, in particular, from the sex act.

The erotic, sensual nature of *Celestina* reaches its peak through body images, and paralinguistic discourse. Constant references are made to the senses that arouse erotic impulses. The *carpe diem* is therefore kinetic in nature, as it has constant references to bodily functions. It is through hearing, for example, that both pleasure and sex are initiated: "¡O bienaventuradas orejas mías que indignamente tan gran palabra habéis oído!" (I;54). "Bullicio" suggests both desire and anxiety:

> Este bullicio más de una persona lo hace; quiero hablar, sea quien fuere... (XII;218)

Calisto identifies Melibea by the pitch of her voice: "...que el dulce sonido de tu habla, que jamás de mis oídos se cae, me certifica ser tú mi señora Melibea. . ."(XII;219). Lovemaking is revealed through "bullicio"; Pleberio is aware of noise in his daughter's bedroom that is an indicator to the reader that Calisto and Melibea are engaging in sexual activity:

> ¿No oyes bullicio en el retraimiento de tu hija?...¿Quién da patados y hace bullicio en tu cámara? (XII;226)

When Melibea waits impatiently for Calisto's arrival in Act XIV, she uses the command "oye" emphatically, because if she listens carefully enough, she will hear her lover arrive:

> Mas oye, oye, oye, que pasos suenan en la calle y aun parece que hablan desotra parte del huerto.(XIV;241)

Calisto enters Melibea's room alone because he has already heard her:

> Quedaos, locos, que yo entraré solo, que a mi señora oigo. (XIV;242)

Even Lucrecia, Melibea's servant, is aware of what Calisto and Melibea are doing as she listens to them with envy:

> (Mala landre me mate si más los escucho. ¿Vida es ésta? ¡Qué me esté yo deshaciendo de dentera y ella esquivándose porque la rueguen...) (XIX;282)

Calisto considers sight to be the cause of his lovesickness, since his eyes are the reason why he was able to see and therefore fall in love with Melibea:

> ¡Oh mis ojos! Acordaos como fuistes causa y puerta, por donde fue mi corazón llagado, y que aquél es visto hacer el daño que da la causa. (VI; 147).

In *Celestina* the characters are constantly gazing at and looking each other over. Bodies are constantly being examined; anatomy becomes a form of social discourse in which the characters give "portraits" of each other through detailed descriptions of the body. Calisto's bodily description of Melibea exemplifies the importance of sight and body in *Celestina*:

> ¿Quién vido en esta vida cuerpo glorificado de ningún hombre, como agora el mío? Por cierto, los gloriosos santos, que se deleitan en la visión divina, no gozan más que yo agora en el acatamiento tuyo. (I;54)

Calisto comments to the others on how nice Melibea's body is: "¿Crió Dios otro mejor cuerpo?" (VI;149). Not only are women the object of male gaze, but females also gaze at females (see Chapter four). For example, Celestina admires Melibea:

> El temor perdí mirando señora tu beldad. Que no puedo creer que en balde pintase Dios unos gestos más perfectos que otros...(IV;120)

It is the color of Melibea's face that reveals to Celestina and to the reader her lovesickness:

> ¿Qué es, señora, tu mal, que así muestra las señas de su tormento en las coloradas colores de tu gesto? (X;197)

It is through the body and bodily functions that Melibea's servant Lucrecia discovers that Melibea is in love, before Melibea expresses this to Lucrecia verbally and despite Melibea's attempt to hide her feelings:

> Señora, mucho antes de agora tengo sentida tu llaga y callado tu deseo. Hame fuertemente dolido tu perdición. Cuanto más tú me querías encubrir y celar el fuego que te quemaba, tanto más sus llamas se manifestaban en la color de tu cara, en el poco sosiego del corazón, en el meneo de tus miembros, en comer sin gana, en el no dormir. Así que contino se te caían, como de entre las manos, señales muy claras de pena.(X;206)

Touch is an important way in which excitement is aroused in the characters. As noted by Read, "petting" occurs, as when Calisto refers to "la noble conversación de tus delicados miembros."[142] This is body language-- the body talks by seeing, feeling, and touching. Celestina pleads with Pármeno to touch Areúsa so he can feel how desirable she is: "Llégate acá,... Retózala en esta cama" (VII; 167). The body speaks by touch; Calisto touches both the clothes and body of Melibea: "Perdona, señora a mis desvergonzadas manos, que jamás pensaron de tocar tu ropa con su indignidad y poco merecer; agora gozan de llegar a tu gentil cuerpo y lindas y delicadas carnes" (XIV;243). It seems that touch competes with verbal artifice:

---

142 Read, *Birth* 74.

¿cómo mandas a mi lengua hablar y no a tus manos que estén quedas?...
Mándales estar sosegadas y dejar su enojoso uso y conversación
incomportable. Cata, ángel mío, que así como me es agradable tu vista
sosegada, me es enojoso tu riguroso trato; tus honestas burlas me dan
placer, tus deshonestas manos me fatigan cuando pasan de
lugar...(XIX;281-2)

Feeling and holding Melibea also gives Calisto the feeling of possession: "En
mis brazos te tengo y no lo creo" (XIV;242.)

The *cordón* and its symbolic meaning also enter into nonverbal body
imagery.[143]

Y mándame mostrar aquel santo cordón, que tales miembros fue digno de
ceñir. ¡Gozarán mis ojos con todos los otros sentidos, pues juntos han sido
apasionados! ¡Gozará mi lastimado corazón, aquel que nunca recibió
momento de placer después que aquella señora conoció! Todos los
sentidos le llagaron, todos acorrieron a él con sus esportillas de trabajo.
Cada uno le lastimó cuanto más pudo; los ojos en vella, los oídos en oilla,
las manos en tocalla. (VI;144-5)

Within the context of body language, the *cordón* plays a masturbatory role,
since upon seeing and especially touching it, Calisto gets aroused: "y mándame con
todos los sentidos." (185) For Calisto the girdle has become a sort of fetish,[144] a
surrogate that has become a precondition for pleasure-- it temporarily replaces the
"real thing." In addition, it appeals to several of the senses: sight, hearing, and touch.

Finally, other paralinguistic features such as crying also have sexual
overtones. Melibea speaks of "llorar de plazer," again a binary opposition that implies
sexual force. Body scent is also arousing; Calisto refers to Melibea's scent as
"saludables olores"(XII;221).

The above examples of nonverbal means of communication reveal a
transformation of bodies into embodiments of carnality. Woman's body, as we shall
see in greater detail in Chapter four, makes a statement about freedom. Women define
themselves sexually as "venidas a haber placer" through their bodies. A new poetics
of the body is created in which corporal censorship and taboos have been lifted. Not

---

143 See Alan D. Deyermond 25-30.
144 On fetishes see Kaja Silverman, *The Acoustic Mirror: The Female Voice in Psychoanalysis
and Cinema* (Bloomington: Indiana UP, 1988) 13-22; Toril Moi, ed., *The Kristeva Reader* (New
York: Columbia UP, 1986) 113; Paul Julian Smith, *The Body* 19.

only do the characters have a lack of inhibition about themselves, but they have ironic awareness of their own unconventionality.

4. Laughter and comical imagery

Finally, another form of *carpe diem* imagery is present in *Celestina*. The delight the characters take in punning and telling sex jokes intensifies even further the *carpe diem* theme.[145] Critics have often overlooked the comical side of *Celestina* and focused more on the tragical, pessimistic aspect of the work.[146]

The abundance of adages, proverbs, and dirty jokes expresses the *carpe diem* philosophy through laughter.[147] Laughter, affirms Bakhtin, is also a component of the lower bodily stratum; it is yet another manifestation of freedom of spirit and speech:

> [Laughter] ... was linked with the procreating act, with birth, renewal, fertility, abundance. Laughter was also related to food and drink and the people's earthly immortality, and finally it was related to the future of things to come and was to clear the way for them. Seriousness was therefore elementally distrusted, while trust was placed in festive laughter.[148]

Perhaps the witty adages and proverbs that express the *carpe diem* theme in *Celestina* are yet another facet of *carpe diem* imagery; the message of these humorous forms is a possible answer to what Horace himself asked: "What prevents him who says the truth from laughing?"[149]

The characters in *Celestina* are well aware of their use of adages and proverbs, since several proverbs are cited with introductory words such as "refrán viejo es....," "proverbio antiguo es...," and "como dicen...." The deliberate use of puns is yet another mode of expressing the *carpe diem* theme. In fact, most of the *carpe diem*

---

145 For more on proverbs see José Gella Iturriaga, "444 Proverbs in *La Celestina*," *ACTAS* (Barcelona, 1977) 245-288. "Tan solo una obra de la literatura española, *El Ingenioso Hidalgo Don Quijote de la Mancha*, contiene más refranes que la *Tragicomedia de Calisto y Melibea*"; Mac E. Barrick,"El 446 Refrán de Celestina," *Celestinesca* 7 (1983): 13-15; Fernando Cantalapiedra, "Los refranes en Celestina y el problema de su autoría," *Celestinesca* 8 (1984): 49-53; Barbara Riss Dubno and John K. Walsh. "Pero Diaz de Toledo's Proverbios de Seneca and the composition of *Celestina*, ACT IV," *Celestinesca* 2 (Mayo, 1987): 3-12.

146 Dorothy Sherman Severin, "Humor in *La Celestina*," *Romance Philology* 32 (1978-79): 274-291; Severin, *Tragicomedy* 63-80.

147 Frantz 10. Says that in the Renaissance "...groups just got together to exchange their latest jokes, present a rebald, farce, or read a bawdry book..."; For a study of sexual humor see Gershon Legman, *Rationale of the Dirty Joke: An Analysis of Sexual Humor* (New York: Bell, 1975.); Robert A. George and Allan Dundes, "Toward a structure of the riddle," *Journal of American Folklore* 76 (1963): 113.

148 Bakhtin, *Rabelais* 95.

149 Bakhtin, *Rabelais* 100.

arguments that have been analyzed in Chapter two, are in the form of proverbs. These proverbs are authoritative in nature because of their ancient origins and the characters' awareness that they are using proverbs, which are also comical and light, creating a tone similar to that of Erasmus' *Praise of Folly*. However, in *Celestina* the function of the *carpe diem*-oriented proverb is mainly that of initiating the *carpe diem* call. It is the basis of Celestina's *carpe diem* argument: "Ganemos todos, partamos todos, holguemos todos. Yo te le traeré manso y benigno a picar el pan en el puño y seremos «dos a dos» y, como dicen, «tres al mohino»" (I;79).

Celestina also employs *carpe diem*-oriented proverbs to express the idea of sharing both material and carnal goods: "El placer no comunicado no es placer" (VIII;172). In addition, proverbs convey the biological need that women and men have for each other: "Que, cuando nace ella, nace él, y cuando él, ella" (VII;162); "«con mal está el huso, cuando la barba no anda de suso»",(IV;119) the need to fulfill sexual desires, and the overall need that humans have for diversions in life: "«que no de solo pan viviremos?»" (IV;118); "«entre col y col, lechuga»" (VI;135).

Finally, Celestina employs *carpe diem* proverbs to express the uselessness of unnecessary worrying and concern over past events, as she emphasizes the importance of living the moment: "¿tú no ves que es necedad llorar por lo que con llorar no se puede remediar?" (I;82); and "quien menos procura alcanza mas bien" (VI;145).

As mentioned in Chapter two, Celestina's followers, namely Areúsa, reiterate similar proverbs told by Celestina previously. After the death of Celestina, Pármeno, and Sempronio, Areúsa justifies the need to continue life and enjoy: "la tristeza es amiga de la soledad" (XV;257); "Y como dicen: «mueran y vivamos»"(XV;257).

The sexual jokes in *Celestina* are also part of the lower bodily stratum of images. These jokes add humor to the sexually suggestive language in *Celestina*. They represent the presence of "bawdy language." In Act I, for example, Sempronio tells a sex-oriented joke in which "ximio" is associated with sexual appetite:[150] "Lo de tu abuela con el ximio, ¿hablilla fue? Testigo es el cuchillo de tu abuelo" (I;62).

The characters themselves laugh at the sexual jokes, as in the following scene in Act I, which provokes laughter:

---

150 This joke has been studied by numerous critics. See for example, Samuel G. Armistead and Joseph H. Silverman, «Algo más sobre "Lo de tu abuela con el ximio"» (*La Celestina I*): Antonio de Torquemada y Lope de Vega», *Papeles de Son Armadans* 69 (1973): 11-18.

> Celestina. ...Llégate acá, putico, que no sabes nada del mundo ni de sus
> deleites. ¡Mas rabia mala me mate, si te llego a mí, aunque vieja! Que la
> voz tienes ronca, las barbas te apuntan. Mal sosegadilla debes tener la
> punta de la barriga. Pármeno. ¡Como cola de alacrán! (I;82)

In this passage reference is made to reproductivity, to copulation, pregnancy,
and phallocentricity-- "cola de alacrán" signifies penis.

We see sexual laughter again in the play on words in the following passage:

> Celestina. ...Pocas mataduras has tú visto en la barriga.   Sempronio.
> Mataduras no; mas petreras sí. (I;70)

Lastly, Calisto uses a graphic pun in response to Melibea's question:

> ¿Qué provecho te trae dañar mis vestiduras? ...Señora, el que quiere
> comer el ave, quita primero las plumas(XIX;282).

This passage underscores once again the importance of laughter in the form
of puns and sexual jokes within the *carpe diem* system of imagery in *Celestina*.

Chapter Four

The *carpe diem*: theme in *Celestina*: a feminist call

The ideological implications of *Celestina* have long been a subject of polemic both among Fernando de Rojas' contemporaries and among modern critics. Diverse and frequently diametrically opposed theories apropos of the social and ideological intentions of *Celestina*, in addition to the work's ambivalent literary genre and its dubious authorship, all have contributed to making *Celestina* an enigmatic work.[151]

Fernando de Rojas himself alludes to the diverse intentions of his work in the "prólogo" of *Celestina*:

> ...no quiero maravillarme si esta presente obra ha sido instrumento de lid o con- tienda a sus lectores para ponerlos en diferencias, dando cada uno sentencia sobre ella a sabor de su voluntad, unos decían que era prolija, otros breve, otros agradable, otros escura; de manera que cortarla a medida de tantas y tan diferentes condiciones a solo Dios pertenece.(50)

The author is also well aware of the ambivalent literary genre of *Celestina*, which has been classified as both tragedy and comedy:

> El primer autor quiso darle denominación del principio, que fue placer, y llamóla comedia. Yo viendo estas discordias, entre estos extremos partí agora por medio la porfía, y llamóla tragicomedia.(51) [152]

---

151 For a discussion of the literary genre of *Celestina*, see Gilman, *The Art*, 3-16; Lida, *La Originalidad*, 11-26; Severin, "Fernando de Rojas and *Celestina*: The Author's Intention from Comedia to *Tragicomedia de Calisto y Melibea*," *Celestinesca* 5 (Mayo, 1981): 1-5; Severin, "Cota, His Imitator, and *La Celestina*: The Evidence Re-examined," *Celestinesca* 4 (1980): 3-8; Severin, "A Minimal Word-Pair Study of 'Celestina': More Evidence about the Authorship of Act I," *Celestinesca* 7 (1983): 11-12; Fernando Ruiz Ramón, "Notas sobre la autoría del Acto I de *La Celestina*," *Hispanic Review* 62 (1974): 431-35.

152 See Gilman, *Art*, 3 "His account of its birth had such an atmosphere of mystery that successive generations of readers have doubted not only his identity but also (and this is a doubt which is far more corrosive) that of the work itself."

Rojas' contemporaries also held contradictory opinions with regard to the literary value of *Celestina*. Cervantes, for example, eulogizes *Celestina* as "divino si encubriera más lo humano."[153] If Golden Age writers such as Cervantes displayed deferential attitudes towards *Celestina*, others were scandalized by the work. Such is the case with the sixteenth-century humanists Antonio de Guevara and Juan Luis Vives, who derogatorily characterize *Celestina* as a "libro pestífero."[154] Whatever differences existed among Golden Age critics, Renaissance readers of the work did not take *Celestina* seriously, since it was perceived as a funny book.[155]

In spite of the diversity of interpretations, *Celestina* should not be viewed as enigmatic, but as a text capable of generating a plurality of codes. In the wake of post-structuralism, the text is viewed as generating a plurality of meanings and interpretations. This concept of plurality is expressed by Roland Barthes in his analysis of narrative structure *S/Z*, where he rejects

> ...both the quest for a single model adequate for all narrative, and the desire to impose meaning on a text in the name of 'interpretation'..."totalizations" and "sources of luminous truths."[156]

In an effort to comprehend the diverse ideological implications of *Celestina*, five principal theories concerning the ideological intentions of the novel will be summarized, followed by an analysis of the ideological intentions of *Celestina* as related to the *carpe diem* concept.

According to the traditional ideological interpretations of *Celestina*, this work has been classified as moral-didactic, religious, socioeconomic, and existentialist.[157] First, *Celestina* has often been characterized as a moral-didactic work whose function is to teach the reader a moral lesson through the dramatic representation of men and women in their inordinate pursuits of pleasures.[158] The second major ideological

---

153 Miguel de Cervantes Saavedra, *Don Quijote de la Mancha* I, ed. Martín de Riquer. (Barcelona: Editorial Juventud, 1955) 32.
154 Juan Luis Vives, "Formación de la mujer cristiana," *Obras Completas* I, ed. Lorenzo Riber. (Madrid: Aguilar, 1947) 1003.
155 See Severin, *Tragicomedy* 18.
156 Smith, *Body* 62; Roland Barthes, *S/Z*, trans. Richard Miller (New York: The Noonday Press, 1974)   9-14.
157 For a study of the major critical approaches to *La Celestina*, see Guillermo F. Ayerbe-Pozo, "Cuatro visiones modernas de *La Celestina*," diss., New York U, 1978; On the intentions of *La Celestina* see Severin, *Tragicomedy* 19, where she classifies two main schools of thought of criticism with regard to the ideologicalintentions of the novel: the Judeo-pessimistic and the Christian didactic.
158 Marcel Bataillon, '*La Celestina*,' *selon Fernando de Rojas*; Dorothy Clarke, *Allegory, Decalogue, and Deadly Sins in La Celestina* 3-28; Menéndez y Pelayo, *Orígenes* III (Madrid, 1910); Vicente Cantarino "Didactismo y moralidad en *La Celestina* 3-109; Otis H. Green,

63

interpretation of *Celestina* focuses on Rojas' Jewish ancestry. Critics of this persuasion view *Celestina* as a work that reflects the social decay and historical conditions of a fifteenth-century Spain obsessed by "sangre pura"; these critics thus place the novel within the "converso" context and classify it as Judeo-pessimistic:[159]

> Desde su angustiosa atalaya de hombre en conflicto con la tradición de sus mayores a la que ha tenido que renunciar por fuerza, y con la tradición impuesta, en la que no halla fácil entrada, el converso Rojas observa la sociedad en que no puede integrarse subrayando sarcásticamente sus contrasentidos, sus prejuicios y sus convenciones.[160]

The third view of *Celestina* is proposed by Antonio Maravall,[161] who relates the novel to the socioeconomic crisis of fifteenth-century Spain:

> *Celestina* nos presenta el drama de la crisis y transmutación de los valores sociales y morales que se desarrollan en la fase de crecimiento de la economía, de la cultura, y de la vida entera, en la sociedad del siglo XV.[162]

Maravall argues that the origins of the characters of *Celestina* are rooted in the "alta burguesía," and that the work represents "el primer episodio en la lucha contra la enajenación que constituye el más hondo drama del hombre desde el Renacimiento hasta nuestros dias."[163] Maravall's interpretation approximates the existentialist view set forth by Esperanza Gurza in which she describes the condition of the human being as one of constant alienation and isolation.[164] According to this,

---

Spain and the Western Tradition, vol. 2: 116, 276; Ciriaco Morón Arroyo, *Sentido y forma de 'La Celestina'* (Madrid: Cátedra, 1974.)

159 See Bakhtin, *Estética* 362. "La literatura es una parte inseparable de la totalidad de una cultura y no puede ser estudiada fuera del total de la cultura...El proceso literario es parte inseparable del proceso cultural."

160 Lida, *Dos obras* 23-24; Gilman, *Spain* 19, 160 "Biographically speaking, he [Rojas] was a member of a caste subject to intense scorn and suspicion, forced into a marginal position, and reacting to persecution in a number of characteristic ways."; Orlando Martínez-Miller, *La ética judía y 'La Celestina 'como alegoría* (Miami: Ed. Universal, 1978); Julio Rodríguez Puértolas, "Nuevas aproximaciones en La Celestina," *De la Edad Media a la edad conflictiva: estudios de la literatura española* (Madrid: Gredos, 1972) 233

161 José Antonio Maravall, *El mundo social de 'La Celestina'* (Madrid: Gredos, 1972); Alan Deyermond, "Divisiones socio-económicas, nexos sexuales: la sociedad de *Celestina*," *Celestinesca* 8 (Otoño, 1984) 3-10; For a sociological interpretation of *Celestina*, see Anthony Van Beysterveldt, *Amadís. Esplandián. Calisto. Historia de un linaje adulterado* (Madrid: Porrúa, 1982).

162 Maravall 22-23. Gilman, *The Spain* 383.

163 Maravall 178.

164 Esperanza Gurza, *Una Lectura Existencialista de 'La Celestina'* (Madrid: Gredos, 1977).

the fourth view, *Celestina* is analyzed from an existentialist position, and the characters in the tragicomedy are viewed as part of the tragic condition of human existence.[165]

In her study, Gurza encounters interesting parallels between *Celestina* and the works of modern existentialist writers. Similarities are drawn between two entirely different yet similar epochs-- fifteenth-century Spain, in its socioeconomic crisis, and modern Europe:

> ...trataré de esclarecer los resultados que dé una lectura de *Celestina* con ojos de modernidad. Este acercamiento me parece válido ...hay similitudes entre la época de crisis en que toma vuelo el existencialismo. Su punto principal de contacto es el énfasis en la vida y en la individualidad.[166]

One of the most recent interpretations of *Celestina* is that of Dorothy Severin, who claims that Rojas' intentions were to create a comical work. Severin defines *Celestina* as a parody of the fifteenth-century sentimental novel.[167] It is the view set forth by Severin that is used as the point of departure in the present study of the *carpe diem* in *Celestina.*

In her analysis, Severin redefines *Celestina* as the first modern novel, classifying it as a "parodic sentimental romance in dialogue which is at the same time both tragic and comic."[168] Severin argues that *Celestina* parodies Diego de San Pedro's sentimental novel, *Cárcel de Amor* (1492), in that Calisto is a parody of the courtly lover Leriano, the protagonist and hero of *Cárcel de Amor.*[169] Severin speaks of Rojas' ability to dissect literary sources:

> ...he parodies them, distorts them, satirizes them, and mocks them. His characters are transformations of existing literary clichés, but in their new incarnations they destroy the old conventions and create new ones.

---

165 See Cándido Ayllon, *Perspectiva irónica de Fernando de Rojas* (Madrid: Porrúa, 1984) 5 "Desde la primera escena de *La Celestina* hasta el trágico y desesperado soliloquio final de Pleberio, la Tragicomedia se destaca por la manera original y moderna en que emolean la ironía tanto el autor del primer auto como Fernando de Rojas. Esta visión irónica, que revela una actitud profundamente pesimista del autor, se manifiesta dentro de la obra en el estilo, la estructura, las fuentes, los temas, y los personajes."
166 Gurza 68.
167 See Severin, *Tragicomedy* Chapter 3 "Genre and the parody of courtly love."
168 Severin, *Tragicomedy* 24.
169 See María Eugenia Lacarra, "La parodia de la ficción sentimental en *La Celestina,*" *Celestinesca* 13 (Mayo, 1989): 11-29.

65

A primary target of this process of destruction and recreation is courtly love and the courtly lover....[170]

Rojas therefore "deconstructs" courtly love and the sentimental novel through parody by turning "...traditional material to a new purpose."[171] Not only does Rojas deconstruct the sentimental novel and subsequently courtly love, he also undoes the very same *carpe diem* concept that medieval and Golden Age poets so fully developed. It is through his parodic tendencies that Rojas radically changes the *carpe diem* concept and its ideological implications.

Indeed, *Celestina* was most frequently seen as a funny and bawdy book and as such was perceived as a "scandalous success."[172] However, little did Rojas know that upon parodying the courtly lover and by deconstructing the *carpe diem* theme, he was creating a new definition not only of the *carpe diem*, but of woman--an innovative phenomenon within the scope of Golden Age Spanish literature.

The deconstruction of the *carpe diem* in *Celestina* reveals strong feminist implications. In this part of the study, therefore, the *carpe diem* in *Celestina* will be analyzed as a theme which lends itself to a feminist discussion. Rojas gives us an innovative view of women, in which the *carpe diem* motif serves as a vehicle of feminist expression. Perhaps one of the most essential aspects of post-structuralism, and subsequently deconstruction, is the view of both the critic and the text as being part of a shifting process.[173] We have seen how, according to Bakhtin (*Rabelais* 198), Renaissance ideological and linguistic shifts from higher to lower spheres result in the concept of the lower bodily stratum. The recognition of this shifting process allows a text to be viewed not as a fixed production, but as a dialectical work capable of different interpretations. If Rojas were to be viewed as literary theorist, his text would reveal not only tendencies toward a parody of the sentimental novel, but also the deconstruction or unraveling of certain Renaissance concepts with regard to the *carpe diem*, and subsequently with regard to women.

In order to fully explicate a feminist reading of the *carpe diem* in *Celestina*, it is indispensable to offer a brief overview of feminist theory pertinent to this study. In the first place, it is through an ideological study that the question of *carpe diem* and woman surfaces, since the social construction of gender takes place through the works of ideology. Literature is prescriptive; it is a "discursive" practice in which

---

170 Severin, *Tragicomedy* 21.
171 Severin, *Tragicomedy* 32.
172 Severin, *Tragicomedy* Chapter 2 "The prefatory material: the author's ambivalent intentions." 9-21.
173Smith, *Margin* 5.

social conventions are ideologically complicit.[174] In fact, literature does more than transmit ideology: it actually creates it--it is a "...mediating, molding force in society."[175]

First of all, the concept of Derridean deconstruction is of utmost importance to this study and to feminists owing to its fundamental idea that the discourse of Western metaphysics is founded on an idealized version of males:

> From the beginning of philosophy, men have set themselves up as the central reference point of an epistemology built on a set of hierarchical oppositions in which 'man' (white, Graeco-Roman, ruling class) always occupies the privileged position: self/other, subject/object, presence/absence, law/chaos, man/woman.[176]

Initiated by Socrates and continued by his pupil Plato, the questioning of presuppositions in Western philosophy has influenced modern philosophers such as Nietzsche and Heidegger, who questioned all philosophies repressed by the sovereign Truth, considered by Nietzsche to be "...illusions of which one has forgotten that they are illusions..."[177] The fundamental principles of deconstruction are based on the "Nietzschean Derridean view of Socratic reason as a tyrannizing force of repression."[178] It is in the very notion of challenging Western philosophy that we arrive at a questioning of Western truths concerning woman.

The post-structuralist movement of deconstruction is parallel to the feminist movement, for as feminist Barbara Johnson states: "It seems to me that women are all trained, to some extent, to be deconstructors. There's always a double message, and there's always a double response. The difficulty, for women, is unlearning self-repression and ambiguation and conciliation, and reaching affirmation."[179] Feminist literary criticism therefore has a dual task of both the deconstruction of predominantly male cultures and paradigms, and the reconstruction of Western

---

174Terry Eagleton, *Literary Theory. An Introduction.* (Oxford: Blackwell, 1983) 205.
175 Terence Hawkes, *Structuralism and Semiotics* (Berkeley: U of California P, 1977) 5.
176Ann Rosalind Jones, "Inscribing femininity: French theories of the feminine," *Feminist Literary Criticism,* ed. Gayle Greene and Coppélia Kahn (New York: Routledge, 1985) 81.
177 Cited by Christopher Norris, *Deconstruction: Theory and Practice* (New YorK: Routledge, 1982) 58.
178 Norris 64.
179 Barbara Johnson, interview, *Criticism in Society,* ed. Irme Salusinszky (New York: Routledge, 1987) 152.

67

culture from a female perspective, with the intention of modifying the tradition that has marginalized woman.[180]

Feminist theory thus starts with certain assumptions based on the fundamental binary opposition, masculine/feminine, which according to Derrida implies the subordination of the second element to the first. Feminist theory then attempts to deconstruct or undo these dichotomies.

Following Derrida's lead, both deconstructionists and feminist critics have set out to undo the ruling illusions of Western philosophy. The principle objective of feminist theory, according to Toril Moi, is political in that it seeks to expose and hopefully deconstruct patriarchal practices.[181] Traditional humanism is also part of patriarchal ideology:

> In this humanist ideology the self is the sole author of history and of the literary text: the humanist creator is potent, phallic and male... the text is reduced to a passive, 'feminine' reflection of an unproblematically 'given', 'masculine' world or self.[182]

Feminists should beware of the potential inverted forms of sexism that can occur, as a result of simply replacing masculine patriarchal images in discourse with feminine ones. The difference, however, between a feminist and a non-feminist critic, says Moi, is that the focus of the former on feminine issues is within a formal, political perspective through the careful analysis of works, literary criticism, and institutions-- all of which have been established by males. We should beware recuperating the very same ideology of the system we repudiate, and making feminism a movement too much like the male search for power or the phallocentric order established by "man."

One of the main goals of feminist criticism and a relevant goal for the present study of *Celestina* is an idea set forth by one of the early American feminists, Mary Ellman. In her essay "Images of Women" Ellman looks for female stereotypes in the

---

180 Gayle Greene; Coppélia Kahn, *Making a Difference. Feminist Literary Criticism* (London: Methuen, 1985) 26 "Deconstruction aims to expose and dismantle an epistomology based on the construction of a sovereign subject - man as 'the central reference point of an epistomology built on a set of hierarchical oppositions in which "man" ... always occupies the privileged postion'. Only the undermining of such oppositions, the dismantling of the system that sanctions them, can undo the hierarchical opposition between men and women. In this way an epistemologically radical feminist criticism may be allied with deconstruction in seeking a 'leverage for displacing or undoing the system of concepts or procedures of male criticism' (Culler 1982, 63)."
181 For an excellent introduction to feminist criticism see Toril Moi,*Sexual/Textual Politics* (New York: Routledge, 1985)
182 Moi, *Sexual/Textual* 8.

works of male writers. The task of the present analysis is similar: to examine how Rojas deconstructs female stereotypes in *Celestina*. Ellman also claims that Western culture has been dominated by the male hierarchy because of our tendencies toward sexual analogy: all phenomena are viewed "in terms of our original and simple sexual differences."[183]

French Feminism

This feminist view of *Celestina* is principally based on French feminist theory. I have purposely chosen to apply French feminist theory to my study because of the francofeminist focus on language as patriarchal in nature, and as based on binary oppositions created by male supremacy.[184] The target of French feminist thought is phallocentrism-- emphasis on the phallus as a symbol of sociocultural authority. Influenced by European philosophers such as Nietzsche, Heidegger, Marx, and by Derridean deconstruction and Lacanian psychoanalysis, the French feminists treat textual, linguistic, semiotic, and psychological theory. They also distinguish themselves from their American counterparts in that they defend women's rights to respect their unique female values, for "they reject 'equality' as an overt attempt to force women to become like men."[185] This is an important point for this study since I do not claim that in *Celestina* women attempt to be like men, but rather they extol their femininity and sensuality, and develop and progress as women, both in their character development and their ideologies.

The main theorists that I shall briefly discuss here are post-Freudian psychoanalyst Jacques Lacan, and feminists Hélène Cixous and Luce Irigaray. A brief description of the most pertinent concepts of each theory is given below.[186]

---

183 Cited by Moi, *Sexual/Textual*, 32 from Mary Ellman, *Thinking About Women* (New York: Harcourt, 1968) 6.
184 There have been recent efforts by American scholars also to break with sexist language. Proof of the current attempt to recreate language by undoing sexist language are the numerous publications of non-sexist dictionaries, and the restructuring of basic guidlelines for scholars, requiring them to use non-sexist language. See Francine Wattman Frank, and Paula A. Treichler, *Language, Gender, and Professional Writing: Theoretical Approches and Guidelines for Nonsexist Usage* (New York: The Modern Language Association, 1989).
185 Moi, *Sexual/Textual* 98.
186 I present here relevant points of feminist criticism for the scope of my study.

Jacques Lacan

Lacan theorizes a structuralist version of Freudian psychology. The fundamental concept of Lacanian theory resides in what Lacan titles the Imaginary and the Symbolic Order.[187] The Imaginary Order implies the pre-Oedipal period, in which the child does not yet distinguish its identity from that of the mother. The Symbolic Order is equivalent to the Oedipal crisis, which is related directly to the acquisition of language. It is the father who separates the child and the mother, for the phallus, or the Law of the Father, means separation. When the child's primary repression surfaces in the child's use of language-- when the child says "I am" or "You are," s/he has taken his place within the Symbolic Order. The child only comes into existence because of the repression of desire for the mother. Therefore, "I am," means "I am that which I am not." To speak as a subject is the same as representing the existence of a repressed desire. Lacan says the subject is lack-- that which it is not. Thus Lacanian theory reserves the "I" position exclusively for men. Since women by gender lack the phallus, they hold a negative position both in language and society. Woman is therefore silenced and unheard:

> To enter into the Symbolic Order means to accept the phallus as the
> representation of the Law of the Father, all human culture and all life
> in society is dominated by the Symbolic Order and thus by the phallus as
> the sign of lack. The subject may or may not like this order of things,
> but it has no choice: to remain in the Imaginary is equivalent to
> becoming psychotic and incapable of living in human society.[188]

Also important in Lacan's theory is the Mirror Stage--a point in the Imaginary Order, when the child looks at itself in the mirror. It merely merges and identifies itself with other human beings it sees. There is no separation of self from the Other until the father breaks the mother/child relationship upon the child's entry into the Symbolic Order, which opens the unconscious--self emerges therefore as the result of a repression of desire. Desire, for Lacan, is continuous and can never be satisfied until death.

---

187 For more on Lacan see Juliet Mitchell and Jacqueline Rose, ed. and trans. *Feminine Sexuality: Jacques Lacan and the école freudienne* (New York: W. W. Norton & Company, Inc., 1985).
188Moi, *Sexual/Textual* 100.

Hélène Cixous

The writings of French feminist Hélène Cixous are important for this study, particularly her theory of "patriarchal binary thought," in which she outlines the structure of the phallocentric system.[189] In her work *The Newly Born Woman*, Cixous lists the following binary oppositions:

> Activity/Passivity
> Sun/Moon
> Culture/Nature
> Day/Nature
> Father/Mather
> Head/Emotions
> Intelligible/Sensitive
> Logos/Pathos

These all correspond to the underlying opposition man/woman, and are a result of the patriarchal value system in which each opposition has a negative or feminine side which can be viewed as the powerless one.

Cixous prefers to speak of gradations of "différence" instead of the powerfully absolute binary oppositions typical of structuralists such as Greimas. She derives her idea of "différence" from the deconstructionist Derrida, for whom meaning or signification is not limited to the prison of "binary oppositions." Cixous speaks instead in terms of degrees-- much, more, less, etc.

This is why she views binary oppositions as part of the prison-house of patriarchal language. Cixous opts instead for the Derridean concept of "free play of the signifier," which does not limit meaning to the prison of binary oppositions. She rejects Freudian and Lacanian theories of woman as "that which is not" or "lack"; she also calls for an assertion of the female body as a positive force, and an erotics of writing derived from feminine unconsciousness.

We will see how *Celestina* breaks, for example, with patriarchal binary oppositions, because *Celestina* is an example of what Cixous defines as "feminine texts" or "texts that work on the difference." Works like *Celestina*, for example, "struggle to undermine the dominant phallocentric logic, split open the closure of binary oppositions and they revel in the pleasures of open-ended textuality."[190]

---

189 Hélène Cixous and Catherine Clément, *The Newly Born Woman*, trans. Betsy Wing (Minneapolis: U of Minnesota P, 1986) 63.
190 Moi, *Sexual/Textual* 108.

A point that this francofeminist makes, which is important in a feminist reading of the *carpe diem* in *Celestina* ,is that emphasis should not be placed on the gender of the author. A work which is

> ....signed with a woman's name doesn't necessarily make a piece of writing feminine.and conversely, the fact that a piece of writing is signed with a man's name does not in itself exclude feminity. It's rare, but you can sometimes find feminity in writings signed by men: it does happen.[191]

Feminist readings of works written by some male authors, as is the case with Rojas, reveal images of positive, non-denigrating women characters; these works are thus supportive of feminist theories. Even though Cixous's words may appear extreme, she is speaking of literature as dominated by patriarchal conventions. Rojas, a male author, is one of the few, as we shall see, who, through his innovative depiction of women, reveals keen insight into feminine thought.

Irigaray

Although heavily criticized by Lacanians for her radical position with regard to Freudian psychology, Luce Irigaray's well-known work, *Spéculum de l'autre femme* (1974), has greatly influenced French feminist theory. *Spéculum de l'autre femme* is an analysis of anti-patriarchal criticism of phallocentric discourse. Irigaray postulates a specific feminine language, consisting of female sexual morphology which she calls "parler femme." Irigaray argues that Freud's theory on the sexes, although revolutionary, is a part of the misogynistic rules of Western philosophy. She does not however reject Freudian theory, as it serves as the main part of deconstructing patriarchal discourse. She argues against Lacan's conclusion that woman is perceived as an outsider to language.

Irigaray uses the image of the speculum in the title of her work, as signifying a mirror, whose reflecting images have traditionally been an expression of patriarchal discourse. Moi tells us that according to the Oxford English Dictionary, the term "speculum" has several meanings: first, it is an instrument for dilating cavities of the human body for inspection; and second, it refers to a reflecting telescope. Note also that the original Latin meaning of speculum is from "specere," "to look." I cite here Irigaray's explanation of the mirror:

---

191 Hélène Cixous, "Castration or decapitation?," *Signs* trans. Annette Kuhn, Signs 7 (1981): 41-55.

72

You will have noted, in fact, that what polarizes the light for the exploration of internal cavities is, in paradigmatic fashion, the concave mirror. Only when that mirror has concentrated the feeble rays of the eye, of the sun, of the sun-blinded eye, is the secret of the caves illumined. Scientific technique will have taken up the condensation properties of the 'burning glass,' in order to pierce the mystery of woman's sex, in a new distribution of the power of the scientific method and of 'nature.' A new despecularzation of the maternal and the female? Scientificity of fiction that seeks to exorcise the disasters of desire, that mortifies desire by analyzing it from all visual angles, but leaves it also intact. Elsewhere. Burning Still.[192]

Woman for Irigaray is Man's Other, his negative mirror image. Thus "patriarchal discourse situates woman outside representation as if she were absent." As explained by Paul Julian Smith, women are "caught in the mirror of representation, central to a male perspective but ultimately excluded from it."[193]

Literary genres, situations, and characters have often been defined according to masculine perspectives, which tend to portray females as stereotypes in literature. The argument set forth in this chapter is that the *carpe diem* theme of lyric poetry is a product of patriarchal discourse, as opposed to the *carpe diem* in *Celestina*, which gives a profeminist, positive portrayal of women.

Paul Julian Smith describes Spanish Golden Age poetry as being "massively male..[since] man is the viewer and speaker, woman the object of his gaze and of his amourous discourse."[194] This is true of Spanish Golden age *carpe diem* poetry, where the poet=narrator are both male.[195] Berrio defines the *carpe diem* poem as:

> ...una concepción del mundo en el cual el goce amoroso de la hermosura física de las mujeres adquiere una mera condición instrumental.[196]

The *carpe diem* poetry of the Spanish Golden Age is one of the best examples of female stereotyping that occurs in male literature; in it the praise of woman's beauty is both patriarchal and misogynistic. Derived from traditional Western

---

192 Luce Irigaray, *Speculum of the Other Woman*, trans. Gillian C. Gill (Ithaca: Cornell UP, 1985) 146.
193 Smith, *The Body* 21.
194 Smith, *The Body* 51-52.
195 See Berrio 247. He confirms that the poet=narrator=lover are one and male in gender.
196 Berrio 247.

patriarchal humanism, *carpe diem* poetry, in the depiction of experiences by male poets, portrays woman's role as nothing more than instrumental.

A careful analysis of the *carpe diem* paradigm in Golden Age poetry reveals the systematic use of conventional gendering of the female as symbol of the paradoxical nature of life. Such a view is typical of misogynistic Western philosophy. Below are two poems written by the Spanish Golden Age poets Garcilaso de la Vega and Luis de Góngora, respectively. Despite the chronological gap that exists between the poems, they both employ the *carpe diem* theme: the male poet calls a young, beautiful woman to enjoy her youth by persuading and sometimes even threatening her:[197]

> En tanto que de rosa y d'azucena
> se muestra la color en vuestro gesto
> y que vuestro mirar ardiente, honesto,
> con clara luz la tempestad serena;
> y en tanto que'l cabello, que'n la vena
> del oro s'escogió, con vuelo presto
> por el hermoso cuello blanco, enhiesto,
> el viento mueve, esparce y desordena:
> coged de vuestra alegre primavera
> el dulce fruto antes que'l tiempo airado
> cubra de nieve la hermosa cumbre.
> Marchitará la rosa el viento helado,
> todo lo mudará la edad ligera
> por no hacer mudanza su costumbre.[198]

> Mientras por competir con tu cabello,
> oro bruñido al sol relumbra en vano,
> mientras con menosprecio en medio el llano
> mira tu blanca frente el lilio bello;
> mientras a cada labio, por cogello,
> siguen más ojos que al clavel temprano,
> y mientras triunfa con desdén lozano

---

197 In this chpater, I do not include the metaphysical poetry of Quevedo. Even though he speaks of the existential themes of mortality, time, and death, what is of particular interest here is *carpe diem* expression within the woman/floral motif.
198 Garcilaso de la Vega, "Soneto XXIII," *Poesías castellanas completas*, ed. Elias L. Rivers, 6th ed. (Madrid: Castalia, 1989) 59.

del luciente cristal tu gentil cuello;
goza cuello, cabello, labio y frente,
antes que lo que fue en tu edad dorada
oro, lilio, clavel, cristal luciente,
no sólo en plata o viola troncada
se vuelva, mas tú y ello juntamente
en tierra, en humo, en polvo, en sombra,
en nada.[199]

In the first poem, Garcilaso employs pre-fabricated clichés based on the floral motif that are confined to the parameters of "catachresis".[200] That is, he uses Petrarchan images based on the rose motif in which the rose is the incarnation of both feminine beauty and the fragility of life. In *carpe diem* poetry, lyric is the equivalent of lady and flower: rosa= rosy cheeks, azucena=lily white brow, oro=hair. The anaphoric use of the temporal conjunction "en tanto," intensifies the present beauty of the lady, while the temporal conjunction "antes que," accentuates more the certainty of future unattractiveness and old age.[201] In a highly graphic way, the lady is advised to enjoy youth, "...coged de vuestra alegre primavera...," before the inevitable coming of old age: "antes que el tiempo airado cubra de nieve la hermosa cumbre." She too, like the rose, will wither and die. The juxtaposing of Petrarchan images along with negative mirror images of the lady's future deformity is one example of the patriarchal nature of *carpe diem* poetry; the poet deliberately chooses woman as symbol of an aporiac (self-engendered) concept of the *carpe diem*. Woman in *carpe diem* poetry is, as Irigaray describes, man's negative mirror image, for "patriarchal discourse situates woman outside representation as if she were absent."[202] To recall Paul Julian Smith's words: women are "caught in the mirror of representation, central to a male perspective but ultimately excluded from it."[203]

Smith questions the mimetic value of floral metaphors, claiming that they are distanced, with no real nor direct correspondence to reality. He describes floral metaphors as catachretal and circular in meaning in the sense that comparing a woman to a rose gives the reader no access to reality, for if a woman is a rose then

199 Luis de Góngora, *Antología Poética*, ed. Antonio Carreira, 2nd ed. (Madrid: Castalia, 1987) 101.
200 Smith, *Body* 64. He defines catachresis as "metaphors deprived of primary terms."
201 See Wardropper 64-65.
202 Moi, *Sexual/Textual* 130.
203 Smith, *Body* 21.

75

what is a rose to be compared to? This idea is also expressed by Roland Barthes in *S/Z*: "Woman copies the Book and all bodies are a quotation of that which is already written."[204] Feminine beauty in *carpe diem* poetry has no parallel or referent. Woman is shown as mere ornamental decoration; she is an instrument with which the poet can express this theme.

Proof of the patriarchal tendency in poetry is the fact that in *carpe diem* poetry, male poets have chosen the female gender, represented by the floral motif, to symbolize the universal metaphysical theme of immortality; they focus on woman's beauty, femininity, aging, and decay: "Implicit or explicit in their poetry is their sense of horror at the inexorable, irreversible flight of time: 'tempus fugit irreparabile.'"[205] Time, the essence of life is symbolized in woman.

The traditional *carpe diem* motif is a product of the male patriarchal system in which the male poet both idealizes and denigrates the lady. She is a flower who upon wilting is useless. The *carpe diem* poet thus destroys the woman in spite of his insistence, paradoxically, that she "seize the day," by bombarding her with future images of decay. He is endowing her with beauty and youth and yet depriving her of these at the same time, as if she really had no right after all to enjoy. This idea is parallel to Irigaray's notion of "indifférente":

> Within the masculine order, the woman is indifferent in the sense of
> non-different or undifferentiated because she has no right to her own
> sexual difference but must accept masculine definitions and
> appropriations of it...As a consequence, she is indifferent in the sense
> of detached or remote because of the importance of her position.[206]

The idea of woman as deprivation can be observed in other disciplines outside of literature in the Golden Age. "Physiologically, woman is held to be an imperfect version of the male: while man is hot, woman is cold. She consequently lacks the moral qualities associated with high body temperature: courage, liberality, honesty."[207] Since the male poet addresses himself to an unknown, non-identified female, the woman is never imagined to experience "jouissance." Despite the constant *carpe diem* call, it is man who speaks of enjoyment, based on the assumption that he

---

204 Smith, *Body* 62.
205 See Wardropper 75.
206 Luce Irigaray, *The Sex Which is Not One*, trans. Catherine Porter (Ithaca: Cornell UP, 1985) 220.
207 Smith, *Body* 50. For more on Renaissance woman see Ian McLean, *The Renaissance Notion of Woman* (Cambridge:Cambridge UP,1980) as cited by Smith, *Body* 50 footnote 15.

has experienced "jouissance." It appears that as far as Spanish literature is concerned, no female poet addresses herself this way to a man.[208]

In the second poem, by Góngora, the male poet's tone is more bitter, cynical, and threatening than that of Garcilaso's. This poem is highly descriptive and graphic; the woman's body is reconstructed anatomically--each point of beauty is enumerated. Woman's body is represented through imagery drawn from the same pre-existing petrarchan codes of *carpe diem* poetry:

> oro=cabello
> blanca=frente
> lilio=bello
> gentil=cuello

The fragmentary representation of women through conventionalized images of the female body in Renaissance love poetry shows the poet's attempt to defend himself against the threat of the female "other" by reducing her/it to separate manipulable body parts: "cuello," "labio," "cabello," "frente." Góngora's mode of expression is highly intense: the temporal conjunction "mientras" used at the beginning of the first two stanzas accentuates both human temporality and feminine and human fragility. The poet threateningly calls woman to enjoy, through the use of the imperative "goza," warning her of the coming of old age in the line, "no solo en plata o viola troncada/se vuelva," referring to graying hair and the wilting flower image that implies death. After the death image the poet continues this graphic visualization of future deformity by reducing the lady to nothing: "en tierra, en humo, en polvo, en sombra, en nada." These five different nouns in the closing lines basically express and reiterate the same "nothing" concept.

The physical description of feminine beauty in *carpe diem* poetry does not serve to praise women's beauty as it sought to do or as it could appear on the surface. It is not only a way of reducing woman to nothing or "indifférente" and depriving her of "jouissance"; it is also a way in which the male poet can display power and authority both as poet and male. The *carpe diem* motif in poetry is one of distorted images, which resembles the speculum as defined by Irigaray--a "curved, distorting mirror which seeks to shed light on woman's darkness and integrates her supposed formlessness."[209] Woman is therefore "caught in the mirror of representation,

---

208 Smith, *Body* 52 "There is no Spanish equivalent of Louise Lebé or Gasparci Stampa, a woman poet to speak in praise of man as object of desire."
209 Moi, *Sexual/Textual* 133.

central to a male perspective but ultimately excluded from it."[210] The *carpe diem* can be characterized by the words of Edward Said, as reflecting the male values of "succession, paternity, and hierarchy."[211]

The authoritative tone of the *carpe diem* poem is illustrated by the use of the imperatives "goza," "mira," and "coge," and by the overall authoritative, prescriptive tone that the poet employs upon giving *carpe diem* advice. *Carpe diem* poetry, like all patriarchal literature, reflects the theme of female submission to male authority, culture, and phallocentricity. It also reflects what Mary Ellman describes as the "assertive, authoritarian mode in which men traditionally write."[212]

Another male mode of expressing authority is through the gaze. Defined according to the Freudian theory of sexual difference: "...based on the visibility of difference; it is the eye that decides what is clearly true and what isn't."[213] As Paul Julian Smith observes, the male in Spanish literature is both viewer and speaker and the look, or in Lacanian terms, the gaze, is an important form of male "jouissance" in *carpe diem* poetry. It is therefore not coincidental that Góngora places "siguen más ojos que al clavel," referring to the lustful eyes of men, in the first part of his poem where he is "praising" the woman's youthful sensuous beauty. "Ojos" implies the eyes of all men; it is through his gaze that the male, and the poet, not only enjoys, but as spectator excludes himself from the aging and decaying process. His "jouissance" lies in his authority and control both of his text and of woman. Irigaray defines the gaze as phallic oriented where "scopophilia" or the love of looking gives the male power over the genital/woman/sex of the female.[214] The poets' gaze represents both past, present and future experiences to come.

The eyes are instruments with which the subject can satisfy his desire. In Lacan's essay "Of the Gaze as Objet Petit,"[215] the desire to gaze signifies the subject's search for fantasy. The eyes are the instruments with which the subject executes his drive. The eye is therefore both an organ of perception and of pleasure. It forms part of the Symbolic Order, and the gaze perceives a fantasy. We see that in *carpe diem*

---

210 Smith, *Body* 21.

211 Edward Said, *Beginning: Intention and Method* (New York: Basil Books, 1974) 162.

212 Ellman 166.

213 Moi, *Sexual/Textual* 132.

214 The Freudian theory of sexual difference is based on visibility as perceived through the eye. Freud accentuates the nothingness of women in that men have a visible sexual organ, the penis, and women do not so therefore are perceived as an absence from the male norm.

215 See Jacques Lacan, *The Four Fundamental Concepts of Psychoanalysis*, trans. Alan Sheridan Harmondsworth (London: Hogarth, 1977) 67-119.

poetry, despite the call to woman to enjoy, she is always deprived of any "jouissance" because she is reduced to "indifférente" or nothing. It is the male who enjoys by recollections of past experiences that the evocation of woman's beauty triggers in his mind, and by the desire he finds in his gaze on the female-- an act of pure narcissism. *Carpe diem* poetry is a narcissistic effacement of women.[216] The woman is the male's fantasy, the object of his gaze as he describes her body in minute detail. *Carpe diem* poetry is a seduction of a nonexistent female by the male. The tyrannical male gaze on woman encloses woman in the *carpe diem* poem/prison of binary oppositions.

Just as the speculum reproduces through distortion, the male gaze on female in *carpe diem* poetry is yet another part of the phallic instrument. Woman in *carpe diem* poetry is left outside, she is "absence" and thus portrays "negativity."[217] This distorting, negative, speculum locks and imprisons woman in binary oppositions such as young/old which have all been predetermined by the male patriarchy. The rhetorical devices of contrast and antithesis all have misogynistic repercussions.

It has been observed in this part of chapter four that the male poet and subsequently *carpe diem* poetry are ruled by patriarchal order, where through sexual/textual representation, women are reduced to non-existent forms of "indifference." We shall see how the *carpe diem* theme in *Celestina* differs from that of lyric poetry in that it deconstructs or undoes previous *carpe diem* conventions and shows woman's experience-- one of the main objectives of feminist criticism. Rojas' view as feminist theorist has much in common with the ideas of the French feminists in that women as portrayed by both do not deny or minimize their femininity, but they extol it as a virtue.

One of the most intriguing and progressive aspects of *Celestina* is the innovative way in which Rojas treats both the *carpe diem* theme and, subsequently, his portrayal of women. In fact, *Celestina* could be perceived as being part of a model currently under way in which theorists are arguing that feminism as a mode of thought emerged as early as the fifteenth century in Italy. These theorists view Renaissance feminism as a feature of a broadly revisionist movement that regarded the medieval model of creation as static and hierarchical. Instead, the revisionists favored a model that was dynamic and relational.[218]

---

216 See Lacan 102.
217 Moi, *Sexual/Textual* 133.
218 Constance Jordan, *Renaissance Feminism: Literary Texts and Political Models* (Ithaca: Cornell UP, 1990).

Despite the fact that Rojas is a male author, he has produced a "feminine" writing. A feminist reading of *Celestina* reveals an attitude of disconformity with the patriarchal codes of medieval and Golden Age literature. Rojas does not follow the mainstream of sexual and socio-literary conventions of Golden Age Spain. In particular, the *carpe diem* call in *Celestina* differs radically from the patriarchal *carpe diem* call typical of Spanish Golden Age lyric poetry, in which, as we have seen, the male=poet=spectator, despite his call to the woman to enjoy, is the sole initiator/recipient of pleasure. His call results in the denigration and reduction of woman to "nada." In addition, the *carpe diem* has traditionally been viewed as didactic in that it is considered to have a wisdom-imparting function.[219] Rojas, however, gives a new message to the *carpe diem* where the didactic intention in *Celestina* is a call to liberate woman.

Whereas in *carpe diem* poetry, according to Lacanian terminology, women "n'existe pas," what is perhaps the most innovative feature of the *carpe diem* theme in the prose of *Celestina* is that Rojas (male author) has selected a female *carpe diem* caller, thus granting woman full authority in a task traditionally performed, in poetry, by a male. In addition, Celestina's *carpe diem* message to enjoy youth and carnal pleasures is directed to both female and male, thus rendering it a gesture towards androgyny. The ungendering of the *carpe diem* call in Rojas' *Celestina* is highly significant in terms of the feminist struggle, the main goal of which is to deconstruct the denigrating fundamental binary opposition, masculine/feminine. Rojas achieves this through his androgynous *carpe diem* call, implying that the warning to enjoy youth and the fear of the brevity of life are inclusive of both sexes. In Celestina's *carpe diem* call, men are not mere spectators of future deformity and destruction, for they too are included and will ultimately experience decay like all human beings. In *Celestina* the *carpe diem* call does not discriminate sexually. It offers a possible solution to Derrida's question: "What if we were to approach... the area of a relationship to the Other [woman] where the code of sexual marks would no longer be discriminating?"[220]

Celestina's *carpe diem* call is a fifteenth- century version of "women's liberation," in which woman is no longer portrayed as passive; to use Hélène Cixous' term, she is no longer "indifférente." Women are not only called to enjoy; they do, indeed, experience "jouissance." Whereas the *carpe diem* motif in lyric poetry serves

---

219 Gilhead 136.
220 Jacques Derrida, interview with Christie V. McDonald, "Choreographies," *Diacritics* 12 (1982): 66- 76.

as an instrument that male poets employ to both denigrate woman and express the transient nature of life, the *carpe diem* theme in *Celestina* serves as a catalyst for woman's repudiation of debilitating patriarchal values. The *carpe diem* message is therefore a political statement made by the female characters of *Celestina*.[221] Women in *Celestina* deconstruct phallic myths that have imprisoned and deprived woman of both their being and their autonomy. The *carpe diem* call is matriarchal-- it is an expression of female power; women's *carpe diem* message expresses the desire to free female existence and subsequently female discourse.

With the exception of Catherine Swietlicki's article, "Rojas' View of Women: A Reanalysis of *Celestina*," few feminist readings of *Celestina* exist.[222] Most studies that have treated the portrayal of female characters in *Celestina* have concentrated on the artistic originality and realistic depiction of female characters. Swietlicki acknowledges Rojas's work as feminist: "...the end result of Rojas' view of women as expressed in *Celestina* is a truly feminist outlook which is highly unusual for his era."[223] It is my intention to extend Swietlicki's theory of *Celestina* in the light of modern feminist theories of gender and sexuality.[224]

As Swietlicki has stated, too much emphasis has been placed on the misogynistic and phallocentric dismissal of women in the antifeminist debate between Calisto and Sempronio in Act I, which, just as in the antifeminist literature of the Arcipreste de Talavera and Pedro Torrellas, is typical of views very much in vogue among medieval and Golden Age philosophers and writers.[225]

---

221 Moi, *Sexual/Textual* xiv "The principal objective of feminist criticism has always been political: it seeks to expose, not to perpetuate, patriarchal practices."
222 Swietlicki 1: "Of the numerous critical studies of *La Celestina* which deal with Fernando de Rojas' female characterization and the role of woman as portrayed in his work, none has examined the total effect of the author's treatment of women."
223 Swietlicki 1.
224 See Smith, *Body* 1 "The questions of gender and sexuality are amongst the most important facing the contemporary critic. Yet there has been almost no work attempting to analyze Spanish and Spanish American literature in the light of modern theories of sexuality."
225 Swietlicki 1: "The discussion of women by the author of the first act can, at most, be considered typical of the feminist debates of the epoch in which the misogynist retracts his disparaging remarks. Antifeminist attacks of this sort by laymen are somewhat insincere, and as such, they have been appropriately described as fashionable literary parlor games."; See Berndt, *Amor* 16: "...su actitud [Sempronio] es un reflejo de la larga tradición de antifeminismo en la literatura del occidente." For a general analysis of minsogyny in Western culture see Katherine Rogers, *The Troublesome Helpmate* (Seattle: U of Washington P, 1966). Says female stereotypes in literature can be traced to early Christian and classical Greek literature

As pointed out by Melveena McKendrick, the major debate of the Golden Age focused on whether or not woman was fundamentally evil. Irigaray comments on this enigmatic aspect of women:[226]

> The enigma that is woman will therefore constitute the target, the object, the stake, of a masculine discourse, of a debate among men, which would not consult her, would not concern her, which, ultimately, she is not supposed to know anything about.[227]

Rojas, however, deconstructs the concepts of misogyny and the view of women as enigmatic, which he presents in Act I, in two ways. The first can be observed in the very same act. Just after Calisto has declared himself a Melibean and preceding Sempronio's misogynistic discourse, Sempronio makes void his future attack against woman by telling Calisto, "Haz tú lo que bien digo y no lo que mal hago" (I;60), meaning that Calisto should take Sempronio's verbal advice but not follow his example in his lustful courting of Elicia. As is evident, throughout the remaining twenty acts, Rojas's portrayal of women is indeed "more powerful and outstanding than [that of] men in general."[228] The second way in which Rojas deconstructs the *carpe diem* is in presenting woman's experience as an expression of feminine "jouissance"; because of this, the *carpe diem* becomes an expression of sexual/textual politics.

Areúsa's declaration that women are "venidas a haber placer" implies the inherent right that women have to experience "jouissance." Women in *Celestina* are no longer the silent women of *carpe diem* poetry who, in Lacanian terms, portray "lack." If however, women in *Celestina* are not silenced, they differ also from the "mujer varonil," or

> ...the woman who departs in any significant way from the feminine norm of the sixteenth and seventeenth centuries. She can take the form of the 'mujer esquiva' who shuns love and marriage, the learned woman, the usurper of man's social role, the woman who wears masculine dress..."[229]

---

226 Cited by Swietlicki, 2; Melveena McKendrick, *Woman and Society in the Spanish Drama of the Golden Age: A Study of the "Mujer Varonil"* (Cambridge: Cambridge UP, 1974).
227 Luce Irigaray *Speculum of the Other Woman* Trans. Gillian G. Gill (Ithaca: Cornell UP, 1985) 13.
228 Swietlicki 2.
229 McKendrick ix.

While it is true that women in *Celestina* do deviate from the norm, they do not, however, "shun" either love or marriage, in that they love openly and freely and in fact, they remain single by choice. Like the "mujer varonil," women in *Celestina* are intelligent,-- they frequently discuss "manly" issues such as freedom, equality, and religion. What distinguishes them from the "mujer varonil," however, is that they conserve, with the exception of Celestina, their femininity and sensuality, and they definitely do not wear masculine clothes.[230] The term "mujer varonil," thus does not apply to the women of *Celestina*, since by definition it presupposes masculinity as a prerequisite for women who deviate from the norm. As stated in the beginning of this chapter, it is the French feminist theorists who provide the most apt point of departure for the present discussion, for it is their contention that femininity should be extolled and that women should not imitate men. This is exactly what occurs in *Celestina*, where women define themselves according to their distinctively sensual femininity.

The women of *Celestina* are unique because of the degree of their self-awareness and self-possession: "Por esto me vivo sobre mí, desde que me sé conocer. Que jamás me precié de llamarme de otro, sino mía." They have defined themselves both sexually and sociologically, in their election of their profession and lifestyle. Rojas does not threaten women with images of their future deformity as the poet of *carpe diem* poetry does. The only one who regrets the loss of youth and who speaks of old age is Celestina, who is already aged anyway. She is the *carpe diem* caller; she is aware of her own aging process. The *carpe diem* call to enjoyment not only permits women in *Celestina* to break from the culture of patriarchal silence; it also enables them to experience "experience"--a phenomenon crucial to any women's movement. If experience can be defined as a "...'process' by which, for all social beings, subjectivity is constructed...[and by which] one places oneself or is placed in social reality...,"[231] then the *carpe diem* is an experience which places women in a world of experiencing. Through the *carpe diem* philosophy, women are able to construct their own "écriture feminine" or "parler femme". They communicate with each other, criticize each other, and reflect on their own being.[232]

---

230 For a feminist analysis of Celestina's masculinity see Mary S. Gossy, *The Untold Story: Women and Theory in Golden Age Texts* (Ann Arbor: U of Michigan P, 1989) 19-56.
231 See Teresa de Lauretis, *Alice Doesn't: Feminism, Semiotics, Cinema* (Bloomington: Indiana UP, 1984) 159.
232 See Virginia Woolf, *A Room of One's Own* (London: 1929, 1977). She points out that women are rarely portrayed in relation to each other in works by male authors.

Women who are "venidas a haber placer" imply that they have experienced "jouissance". They reveal that they have experienced sexual pleasure. The French word "jouissance" (enjoyment) is employed because of its specific reference to female sexual climax, which is what gives woman her free sense of being:

> This pleasure ["jouissance"], when attributed to a woman, is considered to be a different order from the pleasure that is represented within the male libidinal economy often described in terms of the capitalist gain and profit motive. Women's jouissance carries with it the notion of fluidity, diffusion, duration. It is a kind of potlatch in the world of orgasms, a giving, expending, dispensing of pleasure without concern about ends or closure.[233]

An interesting parallel is the medieval and Renaissance idea that women enjoy intercourse more than men, in fact doubly, because the nature of their "jouissance" is longer.[234]

Through "jouissance," women free themselves from the prison of patriarchy—women in *Celestina* have ownership of their own body. "Jouissance" in *Celestina* symbolizes the transition from the traditional role of woman as "object of exchange within a male economy" to a role in which they enjoy "...freedom of exchange or reciprocity."[235]

Rojas even deconstructs the phallic-oriented concept of the gaze, which in *carpe diem* poetry, means the lustful, (phallic) gaze of men, who simultaneously gaze at woman and deprive her. In *Celestina*, the gaze is manifestly a form of "jouissance," as can be observed in Act VII:

> ¡Bendígate Dios y señor San Miguel Angel, y qué gorda y fresca que estás! ¡Qué pechos y qué gentileza! Por hermosa te tenía hasta agora, viendo lo que todos podían ver; pero agora te digo que no hay en la ciudad tres cuerpos tales como el tuyo en cuanto yo conozco. No pareces que hayas quince años. ¡Oh quién fuera hombre y tanta parte alcanzara de ti para gozar de tal vista! (VI;162)

---

233 Elaine Marks and Isabelle de Courtivron, *New French Feminisms* (Amherst: U of Massachussetts P, 1980).

234 See Mary Frances Wack, "The Measure of Pleasure: Peter of Spain on Men, Women, and Lovesickness," *Viator* 17 (1986): 173-196. See also Jacques Ferrand, *A Treatise on Lovesickness* trans., ed. Donald Beecher and Masin Ciavollelo (Syracuse: Syracuse UP, 1990).

235 Smith, *Body* 20.

When Celestina gazes at Areúsa's nude body, she enjoys "like a man would" and even regrets not having been a man so that she may unite with her. This lesbian scene opens up the Freudian myth on the gaze as something fundamentally male.[236]

As stated by Swietlicki, what distinguishes Rojas from other fifteenth-century authors is his concern with the social and moral position of woman as opposed to the question of woman as evil or not evil. Not only does Celestina's *carpe diem* call encourage sex outside of marriage; it also enables women in *Celestina* to express themselves politically. Woman as portrayed by Rojas "subverts the political paradigm by her willingness to encourage sexual intercourse outside matrimony--thus avoiding the legitimizing and controlling power of the church and the economic influence of the patriarchal family."[237] All women, with the exception of Melibea's mother Alisa, are single "liberated" women--that is, they are economically independent and content with their unmarried state. They are daring in their attempt to defy the conventions of medieval and Golden Age Spain in their behavior, dress, sexual autonomy, and profession. Areúsa, for example, prefers her lifestyle to that of the "señora" or married woman of society.

Melibea, in addition, choses to remain single. Melibea's choice is particularly interesting in that she theoretically could have married Calisto, since there were no socioeconomic obstacles such as nobility, social class, or religion that would have prevented them from marrying. Melibea opts therefore for free love and subsequently rejects the patriarchal institution of marriage.[238] This rejection is significant because Melibea is directly repudiating the conditions of "doncella cerrada"; she is rejecting virginity and honor, so important in fifteenth-century Spain.[239] Marriage can be viewed as "an expression of the transmission of male

---

236 Severin, *La Celestina* 202, footnote 25. She alludes to the lesbian nature of this scene. See Gossy 41: "Celestina's lesbianism has been bowdlerized by critical inattention".
237 Gossy 38.
238 Otis Green vol. 1: 18, 112; Gilman, *The Art* 62. He says that Melibea "...rejects domesticity, that is to say matrimony or love within time and space."
239 See Lihani 22 "The role of the upstanding medieval woman in general was rather unique, in that the honor of the family rested on her good reputation. The opinion of women held by men was ambivalent, thereby revealing the transitional nature of the period as it edged from the medieval to the Renaissance forms of thinking...the impression that Spanish medieval literature leaves on the reader is that many of the Spanish medieval writers in general, and the didactic ones in particular looked on woman as a deceitful creature." I disagree with Gilman, *Art* 63 that "women are never faced with a moral choice...", because of their deliberate preference for free love.

dominance ... [which] passes through women and settles upon men."[240] The concepts explained in Gossy's fascinating study on the hymen can be applied to Rojas' deconstruction of the virginity myth; as Gossy explains, the hymen is really not an indication of virginity.[241] Melibea's repudiation of marriage implies subsequently the rejection of childbearing within the marriage institution, in which woman is, as pointed out by Rubin, the passive object of male activity in the marital exchange. Within marriage, women are the instruments through which men continue their lineage. By remaining single, Melibea rejects the patriarchal marital vow, "I now pronounce you man and wife," in which "'man'" refers to the essence of a male being, and the word "wife" describes woman not as a person, in her essence, but as a dependence... simply as a relational sign."[242]

By questioning the institution of marriage, women in *Celestina* portray themselves as free, autonomous beings. In *Celestina*, the women do indeed provide role models as they instill a positive sense of feminine identity by portraying women who are self-actualizing, whose identities are not dependent on men. At first glance, the preceding statement may be perceived as contradictory in view of the entire fabric of Celestina's operation, as well as the profession of the prostitutes Areúsa and Elicia which depends on men. However, as Swietlicki has pointed out, "...these women are not conscious of their subservience...they feel extremely free."[243] Rojas does not portray the two prostitutes in a position of degradation vis à vis males. On the contrary: Rojas deliberately places these women in a world of prostitution, conventionally dominated by men, in order to show how capable they are of dealing with men and controlling situations. The prostitutes Areúsa and Elicia, are not merely reduced to exchange value, because they enjoy; they are not victims of their circumstances. Rojas purposely places these free women in a patriarchally dependent atmosphere, thus deconstructing the conventional concept of prostitution as a form of female degradation. Rojas inverts the prostitution paradigm by

---

240 Gayle Rubin, "The Traffic in Women: Notes on the 'Political Economy' of Sex," *Toward an Anthropology of Women* ed. Rayna Rapp Reiter (New York: Monthly Review Press, 1975) 157-210.

241 Gossy 50: "The hymen is not undecidable, that is, the sign of either virginity or marriage or both; it is neither-it is simply a membrane-text...All it tells is that it is and it has nothing to do with the stories told about it."

242 Nell Furman, "The Politics of Language: Beyond the Gender Principle," Greene and Kahn 64. See Gossy 59: "Marriage...is part of the meaning of hymen; and themes of virginity, consummation and marriage attend the untold story in the text." Gossy 49: "The hymen is fictionalized and made to tell the story of the phallus marking women as object; stories of marriage... marriage/copulation or virginity or both...."

243 Swietlicki 5.

portraying Areúsa and Elicia as two free, happy women who are not, in spite of their profession, subservient to men. Areúsa and Elicia are in full control following the deaths of Celestina, Pármeno, and Sempronio. It seems that they regret the loss of their "mother," Celestina, more than the loss of their lovers. With one reiteration of the old *carpe diem* theme, "mueran y vivamos," they resume their normal lives, putting on their "ropas de placer," and continue to enjoy life.

Swietlicki says that Areúsa and Elicia are "outspoken female defenders of their liberty. Areúsa... [is] a voice of class equality... [and] Rojas' choice of two prostitutes as spokeswomen for liberty and equality was unprecedented."[244] Areúsa and Elicia not only make political statements of equality, but they also, through aphorisms such as "las obras hacen linaje," attempt to reconstruct history from a female perspective, and from the bottom up. They tell a story of the anonymous and unaccounted-for women, and not just the women of "alto linaje." Interestingly enough, Areúsa, Elicia, and Melibea, women of diametrically opposed social classes, arrive at the same mode of lifestyle. Rojas has thus removed women, in regard to both class and gender, from their usual marginal position in society. These women have arrived at political consciousness. In fact, Areúsa and Elicia are feminist theoreticians, precursors of Simone de Beauvoir, who make strong political statements in favor of the dignity and position of women of the medieval working class.[245] Interestingly enough, the portrayals of Areúsa and Elicia as feminist theoreticians parallels results from recent studies by feminist historians concerning the socio-political and economic status of women in the Middle Ages and Renaissance.[246] Attempts have been made by feminist historians to reinterpret the history of women by focusing not on the philosophical and religious debates of the Middle Ages and the Renaissance, but rather on documentation such as legal cases, records of guild organizations, dowries, and accounts of the lives of ordinary women. These historians conclude that despite the

244 Swietlicki 5.
245 Simone de Beauvoir, *Simone de Beauvoir Today. Conversations with Alice Schwartzer 1972-1982.* (London: Chatto, 1984) 32, "...feminists are women—or even men, too—who are fighting to change women's condition, in association with the class struggle but independantly of it as well..."
246 On the status of medieval and Renaissance women, see Eileen Power, *Medieval Woman* ed. M.M. Postan, (Cambridge: Cambridge UP, 1975); Ian Maclean, *The Renaissance Notion of Woman. A Study in the Fortunes of Scholasticism and Medical Science in European Intellectual Life* (Cambridge: Cambridge UP, 1980; Margaret W. Ferguson, Maureen Quilligan, and Nancy J. Vickers, eds., *Rewriting the Renaissance. The Discourses of Sexual Difference in Early Modern Europe* (Chicago: U of Chicago P, 1986; Carol Levin, and Jeanie Watson, eds., *Ambiguous Realities. Women in the Middle Ages and Renaissance* (Detroit: Wayne State UP, 1987); Mary Beth Rose, ed., *Women in the Middle Ages and the Renaissance: Literary and Historical Perspectives* (Syracuse: Syracuse UP, 1986).

patriarchal climate of the Middle Ages and the Renaissance, women of all social and economic classes played an active role both professionally and socially. The political statements made by Areúsa and Elicia, and the awareness of the women characters in *Celestina* of their own female experience, reveal a non-biased image of early Renaissance woman. It can perhaps be perceived as what feminist historians define as a "...swerve away from male bias toward female experience as the center of analysis."[247] In other words, the women in *Celestina* are examples of "...a modern feminist awareness [which] began to emerge in the Renaissance."[248]

Another way in which women in *Celestina* disrupt phallic discourse is through mimeticism or the mimicry of male discourse. Through the constant parodying that occurs in *Celestina*, women mimic courtly love and certain Petrarchan images that are used in *carpe diem* poetry. One example occurs in the passage in which Celestina refers to Areúsa's body as looking like a "perla de oro."(161) Celestina converts two separate images perlas=dientes; oro=cabello, into one grotesque deformation by the juxtaposition of two incompatible images, "pearls of gold."

In conclusion to this part of Chapter four, a point to observe is how the feminine "speculum," or the image of woman in *Celestina*, differs radically from the distorted, narcissistic mirroring of woman in *carpe diem* poetry, where man portrays woman as a false being through disproportionate illusions, as he ultimately uses woman to mirror himself. In *Celestina*, women are no longer seen as man's negative image. Like the Bakhtinian concept of the bodily lower stratum, the new concept in *Celestina* is a view of the world turned upside down. The feminine image seen in *Celestina* is thus the vertical mirror image described by Irigaray:

> ...if the mirror turned vertically, then the concavity makes the countenance appear to be all upside down, and the lower rays are driven upwards and the upper downwards... in a concave mirror with a vertical geneatrix, man may be reflected upside down.[249]

The *carpe diem* mirror in *Celestina* no longer reflects a denigrating distortion of woman, but rather it puts patriarchal order under constant scrutiny. The *carpe diem* mirror in *Celestina* liberates woman. Rojas has deconstructed the *carpe diem* theme in that he makes a positive attempt to alter female stereotypes. Through his particular use of the *carpe diem* theme; he shows how conventional concepts of the

---

247 Mary Beth Rose xvii.
248 Merry E. Wiesner, "Women's Defense of Their Public Role," *Women in the Middle Ages and the Renaissance*, ed. Mary Beth Rose, 1-27.
249 Irigaray, *Speculum* 147-149.

carpe diem and of woman are based on false illusions.The carpe diem call in Rojas is dialectical in nature in that it transforms woman from "nada" into a free being-- a major step toward feminine self discovery.

That is why women in Celestina have ownership over their bodies despite the nature of their profession; they are not subservient to men. Could it be that Rojas has altered the Symbolic Order by allowing woman to become self and by making man the Other through the carpe diem?[250]

There is one last way in which women break with the patriarchal order in Celestina. This is seen in Melibea's suicide. In her pre-meditated, deliberate attempt at reuniting with Calisto, Melibea does not behave according to the courtly tradition in which the man usually takes his life. The "death drive," according to Freud, "... can be worked out only by man, never, under any circumstances by woman." Melibea's suicide reveals her commitment to continue "jouissance" as it represents an attempt at reuniting with her lover after death:

> Algún alivio siento en ver que tan presto seremos juntos yo y aquel mi querido y amado Calisto... Y así contentarle he en la muerte, pues no tuve tiempo en la vida. (288, 292)

Melibea's suicide can be perceived as a violation of the pleasure principle; it is yet another positive attempt on the part of a woman within Rojas' carpe diem scheme to break with the patriarchal order.[251]

---

250 Irigaray, Speculum 144.
251 Gossy 11: "This strategy is analogous to the unacceptable but undeniable autoeroticism habitually sublimated in Western literature in the form of the sadomasochistic triad of death, honor, and romantic love: whether for a god, a nation, or a woman."

Conclusion

There can be little doubt that the *carpe diem* theme forms part of the underlying structure of *Celestina*. Not only does the *carpe diem* act as a catalyst, thus permitting the protagonist Celestina to persuade the other characters to enjoy life, it also forms its own system of *carpe diem* imagery, metaphors, vocabulary, and language. The *carpe diem* theme is so intense in *Celestina*, that sexuality actually replaces textuality.

In this study I have attempted to show how, through the newer theories of Derrida, Cixous, and Irigaray, Rojas ultimately deconstructs the *carpe diem* theme by deliberately displacing the authority of the *carpe diem* caller from its traditional realm of the male poet as can be observed in Spanish Golden Age poetry, to a female caller, Celestina. The *carpe diem* call in *Celestina* is really a political call of persuasion destined to women to liberate themselves from the patriarchal system so common to Spanish Renaissance writings. By rejecting the patriarchal institution of marriage, and by displaying positive non- subservient images of women in the profession of prostitution, conventionally perceived by society as male-subservient, Rojas deconstructs and reconstructs history from a female perspective. The *carpe diem* call to political freedom of both Melibea, a "doncella," and of Areúsa and Elicia, working class women, is an attempt at reconstructing society and male-oriented Spanish Golden Age literature.

Works Cited

Abel, Elizabeth. ed. *Writing and Sexual Difference*. Chicago: Chicago UP, 1982.

Aid, Frances. *Semantic Structures in Spanish: A Proposal for Instructional Materials.* Washington D.C.: Georgetown UP, 1973.

Alexandrian, Sarane. *Histoire de la littérature érotique*. Paris: Seghers, 1989.

Anderson, Bonnie S., and Judith P. Zinsser. *A History of Their Own. Women in Europe from Prehistory to the Present*. vol. Iand II. New York: Harper and Row, 1988.

Arenal, Concepción. *La emancipación de la mujer en España*. ed. Mauro Armiño. Madrid; Biblioteca Jucar, 1974.

Armistead, Samuel G., and Joseph H. Silverman. «Algo más sobre"Lo de tu abuela con el ximio" (*La Celestina* I): Antonio de Torquemada y Lope de Vega»." *Papeles de Son Armadans* (69) (1973): 11-18.

Ayerbe-Pozo, Guillermo F. "Cuatro visiones modernas de *La Celestina*." Diss. New York U, 1978.

Ayllon, Cándido. *Perspectiva irónica de Fernando de Rojas*. Madrid: Porrúa, 1984.

Azar, Inés. "Metáfora, literalidad, transgresión: Amor-Muerte en *La Celestina* y en la Egloga II de Garcilaso." *Lexis* 3 (July 1979): 57-65.

Bakhtin, Mikhail. *The Dialogic Imagination*. Trans. Caryl Emerson and Michael Holquist. ed. Michael Holquist. Austin: U of Texas P, 1981.

---. *Rabelais and His World*. Trans. Hélène Iswolsky. Bloomington: Indiana UP, 1984.

Barrick, Mac E. "El 446 Refrán de Celestina." *Celestinesca* 7 (1983): 13-15.

Barthes, Roland. *S/Z*. Trans. Richard Miller. New York: The Noonday Press, 1974.

Bataillon, Marcel. *La Celestina selon Fernando de Rojas*. Paris: Didier, 1961.

Bazin, André. *What is Cinema?*. Trans. Hugh Gray. Berekely: U of California P, 1967.

Beauvoir, Simone de. *Simone de Beauvoir Today. Conversations with Alice Schwartzer 1972-1982*. London: Chatto, 1984.

---. *Le deuxième sexe*. Paris: Gallimard. Trans. Parshley, H.M. *The Second Sex*. Harmondsworth: Penguin, 1972.

Berndt-Kelly, Erna Ruth. *Amor, muerte y fortuna en La Celestina*. Madrid: Gredos, 1963.

---. "Peripecias de un título: En torno al nombre de la obra de Fernando de Rojas." *Celestinesca* 9 (Fall, 1985): 3-46.

Beysterveldt, Anthony Van. *Amadís. Esplandián. Calisto. Historia de un linaje adulterado.* Madrid: Porrúa, 1982.

Black, Max. "Metaphor." *Philosophical Perspectives on Metaphor.* ed. Mark Johnson. Minneapolis: U of Minnesota P, 1981.

Booth, Wayne. "Freedom of Interpretation: Bakhtin and the Challenge of Feminist Criticism." *Critical Inquiry* 9 (1982): 45-76.

Boullosa, Virginia H. "La concepción del cuerpo en *La Celestina.*" *La idea del cuerpo en las letras españolas siglo XIII a XVII.* ed. Dinko Cvitanovic. Bahía Blanca, Argentina: Univ. Nacional del Sur, 1973: 88-117

Bridenthal, Renate, Claudia Koonz, and Susan Stuard, eds. *Becoming Visible. Women in European History.* 2nd ed. Boston: Houghton Mifflin, 1987.

Bristol, Michael D. *Carnival and Theater. Plebeian Culture and the Structure of Authority in Renaissance England.* New York: Routledge, 1985,

Calcraft, R.P. "The Carpe Diem Sonnets of Garcilaso de la Vega y Góngora." *Modern Language Review* 76 (1981): 332-337.

Candelaria, Frederick H. "The Carpe Diem Motif in Early Seventeenth Century Lyric Poetry with Particular Reference to Robert Herrick." Diss. U of Missouri, 1959.

Cantalapiedra, Fernando. "Los refranes en Celestina y el problema de su autoría." *Celestinesca* 8 (1984): 49-53.

Cantarino, Vicente. "Didactismo y moralidad de La Celestina," *ACTAS,* 103-109.

Castro, Américo. *Santa Teresa y otros ensayos.* Madrid: Historia Nueva, 1929.

Castro Guisasola, Florentino Castro. *Observaciones sobre las fuentes literarias de La Celestina.* Madrid: Consejo Superior de Investigaciones Científicas, 1973.

Catullus. *Poems of Catullus.* Trans. Horace Gregory CoviaFriede, Inc., 1931.

Cavallero, Pablo A. "Algo más sobre el motivo grecolatino de la vieja bebedora en *Celestina:* Rojas y la tradición de la comediografía." *Celestinesca* 12 (Otoño, 1988): 5-16.

Cela, Camilo José. *Diccionario secreto.* Madrid: Alianza/Alfaguara, 1987.

Cervantes Saavedra, Miguel de Cervantes. *Don Quijote de la Mancha* I. ed. Martín de Riquer. Barcelona: Editorial Juventud, 1955.

Chaucer, Geoffrey. *The Legend of Good Women.* trans. Ann Macmillan. Houston: Rice UP, 1987.

Cixous, Hélène., Catherine Clément. *The Newly Born Woman.* Minneapolis: U of Minnesota P, 1986.

Clarke, Dorothy C. *Allegory, Decalogue and Deadly Sins in La Celestina*. Berkeley: U of California P, 1968.

Cohen, Ralph., ed. *The Future of Literary Theory*. New York: Routledge, 1989.

Cruz-Saenz, Michelle S. de. "Representación de la *Tragicomedia de Calisto y Melibea:* Compañía Teatro del aire (Madrid), en una gira por los EE.UU. *Celestinesca* 6 (Mayo, 1982): 35-37.

Culler, Jonathan. *The Pursuit of Signs: Semiotics, Literature, Deconstruction*. Ithaca: Cornell UP, 1981.

Curtius, Ernst. *European Literature and the Latin Middle Ages*. Princeton: Princeton U P, 1953.

Damiani, Bruno Mario. *Francisco Delicado*. New York: Twayne, 1974.

---. *Moralidad y didactismo en el Siglo de Oro*. Madrid: Orígenes, 1987.

D'Amico, John F. *Theory and Practice in Renaissance Textual Criticism*. Berkeley: U of California P, 1988.

Davis, Natalie Zemon. *Society and Culture in Early Modern France*. Stanford: Stanford UP, 1965, 1975. (I used 1975 ed)

Derrida, Jacques. Interview with Christie V. McDonald. "Choreographies." *Diacritcs* 12 (1982): 66-76.

Deyermond, Alan D. *The Petrarchan Sources of La Celestina*. London: Oxford UP, 1961.

---. "Divisiones socio-económicas, nexos sexuales: la sociedad de *Celestina*." *Celestinesca* 8 (Otoño, 1984): 3-10.

---. "Hilado-Cordón-Cadena: Symbolic Equivalences in *La Celestina*." *Celestinesca* 1 (Mayo, 1977): 6-12.

---. "El que quiere comer el ave: Melibea como artículo de consumo." *Estudios Románicos dedicados al Profesor Andrés Soria Ortega*. Universidad de Granada, 1985.

Diamond, Arlyn, and Lee R. Edwards ed. *The Authority of Experience: Essays in Feminist Criticism*. Amherst: U of Massachussetts P, 1977.

Dillard, Heath. "Medieval Women in Castilian Town Communities." *Women's Studies* 11 (1984): 115-138.
---. *Daughters of the Reconquest: Women in Castilian Town Society, 1100-1300*. Cambridge: Cambridge UP, 1984.

Dinshaw, Carolyn. *Chaucer's Sexual Poetics*. Madison: U of Wisconsin P, 1989.

du Bois, Page. *Sowing the Body. Pyschoanalysis and Ancient Representations of Women*. Chicago: U of Chicago P, 1988.

Eagleton, Terry. *Literary Theory: An Introduction.* Minneapolis: U of Minnesota P, 1983.

Eliot, T.S. *Selected Essays.* New York: Harcourt, Brace, and World, Inc., 1960.

Ellman, Mary. *Thinking About Women.* New York: Harcourt, 1968.

Ellzey, Susan Gwendolyn. "The Renaissance Rose." Diss. Florida State U, 1973.

Ennen, Edith. *The Medieval Woman.* trans. Edmund Jephcott. Cambridge: Basil Blackwell, 1989.

Escandón, Blanca González de. *Los temas del carpe diem y la brevedad de la rosa en la poesía española.* Barcelona: Universidad de Barcelona, 1938.

Ferguson, Margaret W., Maureen Quilligan, and Nancy J. Vickers, eds. *Rewriting the Renaissance. The Discourses of Sexual Difference in Early Modern Europe.* Chicago: U of Chicago P, 1986.

Felman, Shoshana. *Jacques Lacan...* Harvard up 1987.

Ferrand, Jacques. *A Treatise on Lovesickness.* Trans., ed. Donald Beecher, and Masin Ciavollelo. Syracuse; Syracuse UP, 1990.

Ferrante, Joan M. "Male Fantasy and Female Reality in Courtly Literature." *Women's Studies* 11 (1984): 67-97.

Fothergrill-Payne, Louise. *Seneca and Celestina.* Cambridge: Cambridge UP, 1988.

Foucault, Michel. *Histoire de la sexualité.* Paris: Gallimard, 1976.

Fraker, Charles F. "Declamation and the Celestina." *Celestinesca* 9 (1985): 47-62.

Frank, Francine Wattman, and Paula A. Treichler. *Language, Gender, and Professional Writing: Theoretical Approches and Guidelines for Nonsexist Usage.* New York: The Modern Language Association, 1989.

Frantz, David O. *Festum Voluptatis.* Columbus: Ohio State UP, 1989.

Fraser, T. *Of Time, Passion, and Knowledge.* New York: George Braziller, 1975.

Friedman, Edward H. *The Antiheroine's Voice: Narrative Discourse: Tranformations of the Picaresque.* Columbia: U of Missouri P, 1987.

Friedman, William J. *About Time: Inventing the Fourth Dimension.* Cambridge: Massachusetts Institute of Technology Press, 1990.

Gallery Kovacs, Maureen. trans. *The Epic of Gilgamesh.* Stanford: Stanford UP, 1985.

Gallop, Jane. *Thinking Through the Body.* New York: Columbia UP, 1988.

García Bacca, Juan David. "Sobre el sentido de 'conciencia' en *La Celestina.*" *Revista de Guatemala* 6 (1946): 52-66.

García Berrio, Antonio García. "Tipología textual de los sonetos clásicos españoles sobre el *carpe diem*." *Disposito* 3-4 (1978-79): 243-271.

Gardner, John. *The Poetry of Chaucer*. Carbondale and Edwardsville: Southern Illinois UP, 1977.

George, Robert A., and Allan Dundes. "Toward a structure of the riddle." *Journal of American Folklore* 76 (1963): 113.

Gifford, D.J. "Magical Patter: The Place of Verbal Fascination in *La Celestina*." *Medieval and Renaissance Studies on Spain and Portugal in Honour of P.E. Russell*. ed. F.W. Hodcroft, D.G. Pattison, R.D.F. Pring-Mill, R.W. Truman. Oxford: The Society for the Studies of Medieval Languages and Literature, 1981.

Gilhead, Sarah. "Ungathering 'Gather ye Rosebuds': Herrick's Misreading of the *Carpe Diem*." *Criticism* 27 (1985).

Gilman, Stephen. "The Spanish Writer, Fernando de Rojas." *Year-book of the American Philosophical Society*. (1961): 503-505.

---. *The Spain of Fernando de Rojas: The Intellectual and Social Landscape of La Celestina*. Princeton: Princeton UP, 1972.

---. *The Art of La Celestina*. Madison: U of Wisconsin P, 1956.

Góngora, Luis de. *Antología Poética*. ed. Antonio Carreira. 2nd ed. Madrid: Castalia, 1987.

Gossy, Mary S. *The Untold Story: Women and Theory in Golden Age Texts*. Ann Arbor: U of Michigan P, 1989.

Green, Gayle; Coppélia Kahn, eds. *Making the Difference. Feminist Literary Criticism*. New York: Routledge, 1985.

Green, Otis H. *Spain and the Western Tradition*. 4 vols. Madison: U of Wisconsin P, 1968.

Greimas, A.J. *Semántica estructural*. Madrid, 1971.

Grieve, Patricia E. *Desire and Death in the Spanish Sentimental Romance (1440-1550)*. Newark, Delaware: Juan de la Cuesta, 1987.

Grosz, Elizabeth. *Jacques Lacan: A Feminist Introduction*. New York: Routledge, 1990

Handy, Otis. "The Rhetorical and Psychological Defloration of Melibea." *Celestinesca* 7 (1983): 17-27.

Hawkes, Terence. *Structuralism and Semiotics*. Berkeley: U of California P, 1977.

Heiple, Daniel L. *Mechanical Imagery in Spanish Golden Age Poetry*. Madrid: José Porrúa Turanzas, S.A., 1983.

Hesse, Everett W. "La función simbólica de *La Celestina*." *Boletín de la biblioteca Menéndez Pelayo* 42 (1966): 87-95.

Howell, Martha C. *Women, Production, and Patriarchy in Late Medieval Cities.* Chicago: U of Chicago P, 1986.

Huegas, Pierre. *La Céléstine et sa déscendence directe.* Bordeaux: Institut d'Etudes Ibériques et Ibéro-Américaines de l'Université de Bordeaux, 1973.

Irigaray, Luce. *Speculum of the Other Woman.* Trans. Gillian C. Gill. Ithaca: Cornell UP, 1985.

---. *The Sex Which is Not One,* Trans. Catherine Porter. Ithaca: Cornell UP, 1985.

Iturriaga, José Gella. "444 Proverbs in *La Celestina.*" *ACTAS* Barcelona, 1977: 245-288.

Jaggar, Alison M. and Susan R. Bordo. *Gender/Body/Knowledge: Feminist Reconstructions of Being and Knowing.* New Brunswick: Rutgers UP, 1989.

Johnson, Barbara. Interview. *Criticism in Society.* ed. Irme Salusinszky. New York: Routledge, 1987.

Jones, Ann Rosalind. "Inscribing femininity: French theories of the feminine." *Feminist Literary Criticism.* ed. Gayle Greene and Coppélia Kahn. New York: Routledge, 1985.

---. "Writing the Body." *Feminist Studies* 2 (1981): 247-63.

Jordon, Constance. *Renaissance Feminism: Literary Texts and Political Models.* Cornell UP, 1990.

Joret, Charles. *La rose dans l'antiquité et au moyen age.* Paris, 1892.

Kamen, Henry Arthur Francis. *Spain 1469-1714: A Society of Conflict.* London and New York: Longman, 1983.

---. *Golden Age Spain.* Houndmills, Basingstoke, Hampshire, and London: Macmillan Education Ltd., 1988.

Kauffman, Linda S. *Discourses of Desire: Gender, Genre and Epistolary Fictions.* Ithaca and London; Cornell UP, 1986.

Kirby, Stephen D. "Observaciones pragmáticas sobre tres aspectos de la crítica celestinesca." *Studia hispánica medievalia.* ed. L. Teresa Valdivieso and J. Valdivieso. Buenos Aires: Universidad Católica Argentina, 1988: 71-80.

---. "¿Cuándo empezó a conocerse la obra de Fernando de Rojas como Celestina." *Celestinesca* 13 (1989): 59-62.

Kinser, Samuel. *Rabelais's Carnival: Text, Context, Metatext.* Berkeley: U of California P, 1990.

Kovacs, Maureen Gallery, Trans. *The Epic of Gilgamesh.* Stanford: Stanford UP, 1989.

Labandeira, Amancio Fernández. "En torno a Fernando de Rojas y su biblioteca." *Homenaje a Luis Morales Oliver* Madrid: Fundación Universitaria Española, 1986; 189-220. .

Lacan, Jacques. *The Four Fundamental Concepts of Psychoanalysis.* Trans. Alan Sheridan Harmondsworth. London: Hogarth, 1977.

Lacarra, María Eugenia. "La parodia de la ficción sentimenl en *La Celestina.*" *Celestinesca* 13 (Mayo, 1989): 11-29.

---. "Notes on Feminist Analysis of Medieval Spanish Literature and History." *La Corónica* 17 (1988): 14-22.

Lapesa, Rafael. *Poetas y prosistas de ayer y de hoy: 20 estudios de historia y crítica literarias.* Madrid: Gredos, 1977.

Lauretis, Teresa de. *Alice Doesn't: Feminism, Semiotics, Cinema.* Bloomington: Indiana UP, 1984.

---, ed. *Feminist Studies/Critical Studies.* Bloomington: Indiana UP, 1986.

Legman, Hershon. *Rationale of the Dirty Joke: An Analysis of Sexual Humor.* New York: Bell, 1975.

Lerner, Gerda. *The Creation of Patriarchy.* New York: Oxford UP, 1986.

Lersundi, Fernando del Valle. "Documentos referentes a Fernando de Rojas." *Revista de Filología Española* 12 (1925): 385-396.

---. "Testamento de Fernando de Rojas, autor de *La Celestina.*" *Revista de Filología Española* 16 (1929): 366-383.

Levin, Carol, and Jeanie Watson, eds. *Ambiguous Realities. Women in the Middle Ages and the Renaissance: Literary and Historical Perspectives.* Syracuse: Syracuse UP, 1986.

Lida de Malkiel, María Rosa. *Dos obras maestras de la literatura española. El Libro de Buen Amor y La Celestina.* Buenos Aires: Editorial Universitaria de Buenos Aires, 1966.
---. *La Originalidad Artística de La Celestina.* Buenos Aires: Editorial universitaria de Buenos Aires, 1962.

Lihani, John. "Spanish Urban Life in the Late Fifteenth Century as Seen in *Celestina.*" *Celestinesca* 11 (Otoño, 1987): 21-28.

Lotman, Jurij. *The Artistic Structure.* Trans. Gail Lenhoff and Ronald Vroon. Ann Arbor: U of Michigan P, 1977.

Louison-Lassablière, Marie-Joëlle. "La symbolique florale dans la poésie amoureuse de 1570 à 1620." Thèse de troisième cycle. Université de Saint-Etienne, 1982.

Macdonell, Diana. *Theories of discourse, An Introduction.* Oxford, England/New York: Basil Blackwell, 1986.

97

Maclean, Ian. *The Renaissance Notion of Woman*. Cambridge: Cambridge UP, 1980.

Maeztu, Ramiro de. "*La Celestina*, o el saber," Don Quijote, DonJuan and *La Celestina*: ensayos de simpatía. Madrid: Calpe, 1926.

Maguire, Nancy Klein. Renaissance Tragicomedy: Explorations in Genre and Politics. New York: AMS Press, 1987.

Maravall, Antonio. *El Mundo Social de La Celestina*. Madrid: Redos, 1964.

Marín, Louis. *Food for Thought*. trans. Mette Hjort. Baltimore: The Johns Hopkins UP, 1989.

Marks, Elaine. "Trangressing the (In)cont(in)ent Boundaries: The Body in Decline," *Yale French Studies* 72 (1986): 181-200.

Marks, Elaine, and Isabelle de Courtivron. *New French Feminisms*. Amherst: U of Massachussets P, 1980.

Martínez Marín, Juan. *Sintáxis de la Celestina: La oración compuesta*. Granada: Colección filológica de la Universidad de Granada, 1978.

Martínez-Miller, Orlando. *La ética judía y La Celestina como alegoría*. Miami: Universal, 1978.

McKendrick, Melveena. *Woman and Society in the Spanish Drama of the Golden Age: A Study of the "Mujer Varonil*. Cambridge: Cambridge UP, 1974.

Mendeloff, Harry. "Sharing in *La Celestina*." *Boletín del Instituto Caro y Cuervo* 32 (1977): 173-77.

Menéndez y Pelayo, Marcelino. *Orígenes* III. Madrid, 1910.

Mitchell, Juliet, and Jacqueline Rose, ed., and Trans. *Feminine Sexuality: Jacques Lacan and the école freudienne*. New York: W. W. Norton & Company, Inc., 1985.

Moi, Toril. *Sexual Textual Politics*. New York: Routledge, 1985.

---, ed. *The Kristeva Reader*. New York: Columbia UP, 1986.

---, ed. *French Feminist Thought*. New York: Basil Blackwell, 1987.

Norris, Christopher. *Deconstruction: Theory and Practice*. New York: Routledge, 1982.

Otis, Leah Lydia. *Prostitution in Medieval Society: The History of an Urban Institution in Languedoc*. Chicago: U of Chicago P, 1985.

Pelayo, Menéndez. *Horacio en España*. Madrid, 1885.

Perry, Mary Elizabeth. *Gender and Disorder in Early Modern Seville*. Princeton: Princeton UP, 1990.

---. *Crime and Society in Early Modern Seville.* Hanover: UP of New England, 1980.

Pilotti, Alexander. "A Structural Analysis of Three Sixteenth Century Spanish Carpe Diem Sonnets." Diss. U of Michigan, 1976.

Power, Eileen. *Medieval Woman.* ed. M.M. Postan. Cambridge: Cambridge UP, 1975.

Puértolas, Julio. "Nuevas aproximaciones en *La Celestina.*" *De la Edad Media a la edad conflictiva: estudios de la literatura española.* Madrid: Gredos, 1972.

Read, Malcolm K. *The Birth and Death of Language: Spanish Literature and Linguistics: 1300-1700.* Madrid: José Porrúa Turanzas, S.A., 1983.

Richter, Jean Paul. *The Notebooks of Leonardo da Vinci.* New York: Dover Publications, 1970, vol. 2.

Riss Dubno, Barbara, and John K. Walsh. "Pero Diaz de Toledo's Proverbios de Seneca and the composition of *Celestina,* ACT IV." *Celestinesca* 2 (Mayo, 1987) 3-12.

Rogers, Katherine. *The Troublesome Helpemate.* Seattle: U of Washington P, 1966.

Rojas, Fernando de. *La Celestina.* ed. Buno Mario Damiani. Madrid: Cátedra, 1980.

Rose, Mary Beth, ed. *Women in the Middle Ages and the Renaissance: Literary and Historical Perspectives.* Syracuse: Syracuse UP, 1986.

Rubin, Gayle. "The Traffic in Women: Notes on the 'Political Economy' of Sex." *Toward an Anthropology of Women.* New York: Monthly Review Press, 1975.

Ruiz Ramón, Fernando. "Notas sobre la autoría del Acto I de La Celestina." *Hispanic Review* 62 (1974): 431-35.

Sellers, Susan. ed. *Writing Differences: Readings from the Seminar of Hélène Cixous.* Milton Keynes: Open UP, 1988.

Severin, Dorothy Sherman. *Tragicomedy and Novelistic Discourse in Celestina.* Cambridge: Cambridge UP, 1989.

---. "Fernando de Rojas and *Celestina*: The Author's Intention from Comedia to *Tragicomedia de Calisto y Melibea.*" *Celestinesca* 5 (May, 1981) 1-5.

---. "A Minimal Word-Pair Study of 'Celestina': More Evidence about the Authorship of Act I." *Celestinesca* 7 (1983): 11-12.

---. *Memory in La Celestina.* London: Tamesis, 1970.

---. "Humor in *La Celestina.*" *Romance Philology* 32 (1978-79) 274-291.

---, *La Celestina.* ed. Fernando de Rojas. Madrid: Cátedra, 1987.

Shepherd, W.G. Trans. *Horace: The Complete Odes and Epodes.* By Horace. Middlesex: Penguin, 1983.

Showalter, Elaine. ed. *Speaking of Gender.* New York: Routledge,1989.

Silverman, Kaja. *The Acoustic Mirror: The Female Voice in Psychoanalysis and Cinema.* Bloomington: Indiana UP, 1988.

Smith, Paul Julian. *The Body Hispanic: Gender and Sexuality in Spanish and Spanish American Literature.* Oxford: Clarendon Press, 1989.

---. *Writing in the Margin: Spanish Literature of the Golden Age.* Oxford: Clarendon P, 1988.

---. *Quevedo on Parnassus: Allusion and Theory in the Love Lyric.* London: Modern Humanities Research Association, 1987.

Snow, Joseph T. *Celestina by Fernando de Rojas: An Annotated Bibliography of World Interest 1930-1985.* Madison: The Hispanic Seminary of Medieval Studies, 1985.

---, ed., *Celestinesca.* Athens: U of Georgia Press, 1985-90.

Sponsler, Lucy A. *Women in the Medieval Spanish Epic and Lyric Tradition.* Lexington, Kentucky: The UP of Kentecky, 1975.

Stam, Robert. *Subversive Pleasures: Bakhtin, Cultural Criticism, and Film.* Baltimore: Johns Hopkins UP, 1989.

Swietlicki, Catherine. "Rojas' View of Women: A Reanalysis of *La Celestina.*" *Hispanófila* (September, 1985): 5-6.

Valdés, Juan de. *Diálogo de la lengua.* ed. José F. Montesinos. 6th ed. Madrid: Espasa-Calpe, S.A., 1976.

Vega, Garcilaso de la. *Poesías Castellanas Completas.* Ed. Elias L. Rivers. 6th ed. Madrid: Castalia, 1989.

Vidal, Hernán. ed. *Cultural and Historical Grounding for Hispanic and Luso-Brazilian Feminist Literary Criticism.* Minneapolis: Institute for the Study of Ideologies and Literature, 1989.

Vives, Juan Luis. "Formación de la mujer cristiana." *Obras Completas* I, ed. Lorenzo Riber. Madrid: Aguilar, 1947.

Wack, Mary Frances. "The Measure of Pleasure: Peter of Spain on Men, Women, and Lovesickness." *Viator* 17 (1986): 173-196.

---. *Lovesickness in the Middle Ages. The Viaticum and its Commentaries.* Philadelphia: U of Pennsylvania P, 1990.

Walker, Cheryl. "Feminist Literary Criticism and the Author."*Critical Inquiry* 16 (Spring, 1990): 551-571.

Wardropper, Bruce W. *Spanish Poetry of the Golden Age.* New York: Appleton-Century Crofts, 1971.

Weedon, Chris. *Feminist Practice and Poststructuralist Theory.* New York: Basil Blackwell, 1987.

Weissberger, Barbara F. "Role-Reversal and Festivity in the Romances of Juan de Flores." *Journal of Hispanic Philology* 13 (1989): 197-213.

Wellek, René, and Austin Warren. *Theory of Literature,* third ed. San Diego/New York: Harcourt Brace Jovanovich, 1942.

Welles, Marcia L. "The pícara: Towards Female Autonomy, or the Vanity of Virtue," *Kentucky Romance Quarterly* 33 (1986): 63-70.

Wellington, James Ellis. "An Analysis of the Carpe Diem Theme in Seventeenth Century English Poetry (1590-1700)." Diss. Florida State U, 1955

White, Evelyn B. Trans. *Ausonius,* By Ausonius. Cambridge: Harvard UP, 1949. vol. 2.

Winkler, John J. *The Constraints of Desire. The Anthropology of Sex and Gender in Ancient Greece.* New York: Routledge, 1990.

Woolf, Virginia. *A Room of One's Own.* London: 1929, 1977.

Scripta Humanistica ®

Directed by
BRUNO M. DAMIANI
The Catholic University of America
COMPREHENSIVE LIST OF PUBLICATIONS *

1. Everett W. Hesse, The "Comedia" and Points of View. $24.50
2. Marta Ana Diz, Patronio y Lucanor: la lectura inteligente "en
   el tiempo que es turbio." Prólogo de John Esten Keller. $26.00
3. James F. Jones, Jr., The Story of a Fair Greek of Yesteryear.
   A Translation from the French of Antoine-François Prévost's
   L'Histoire d'une Grecque moderne. With Introduction and
   Selected Bibliography. $30.00
4. Colette H. Winn, Jean de Sponde: Les sonnets de la mort
   ou La Poétique de l'accoutumance. Préface par Frédéric De-
   loffre. $22.50
5. Jack Weiner, "En busca de la justicia social: estudio sobre el
   teatro español del Siglo de Oro." $24.50
6. Paul A. Gaeng, Collapse and Reorganization of the Latin
   Nominal Flection as Reflected in Epigraphic Sources. Written
   with the assistance of Jeffrey T. Chamberlin. $24.00
7. Edna Aizenberg, The Aleph Weaver: Biblical, Kabbalistic, and
   Judaic Elements in Borges. $25.00
8. Michael G. Paulson and Tamara Alvarez-Detrell, Cervantes,
   Hardy, and "La fuerza de la sangre." $25.50
9. Rouben Charles Cholakian, Deflection/Reflection in the Lyric
   Poetry of Charles d'Orléans: A Psychosemiotic Reading. $25.00
10. Kent P. Ljungquist, The Grand and the Fair: Poe's Land-
    scape Aesthetics and Pictorial Techniques. $27.50
11. D.W. McPheeters, Estudios humanísticos sobre la "Celestina." $20.00
12. Vittorio Felaco, The Poetry and Selected Prose of Camillo
    Sbarbaro. Edited and Translated by Vittorio Felaco. With a
    Preface by Franco Fido. $25.00
13. María del C. Candau de Cevallos, Historia de la lengua espa-
    ñola. $33.00
14. Renaissance and Golden Age Studies in Honor of D.W. Mc-
    Pheeters. Ed. Bruno M. Damiani. $30.00
15. Bernardo Antonio González, Parábolas de identidad: Reali-
    dad interior y estrategia narrativa en tres novelistas de pos-
    guerra. $28.00
16. Carmelo Gariano, La Edad Media (Aproximación Alfonsina). $30.00
17. Gabriella Ibieta, Tradition and Renewal in "La gloria de don
    Ramiro". $27.50
18. Estudios literarios en honor de Gustavo Correa. Eds. Charles
    Faulhaber, Richard Kinkade, T.A. Perry. Preface by Manuel
    Durán. $25.00
19. George Yost, Pieracci and Shelly: An Italian Ur-Cenci. $27.50

20. Zelda Irene Brooks, *The Poetry of Gabriel Celaya*. $26.00
21. *La relación o naufragios de Alvar Núñez Cabeza de Vaca*, eds. Martin A. Favata y José B. Fernández. $27.50
22. Pamela S. Brakhage, *The Theology of "La Lozana andaluza."* $27.50
23. Jorge Checa, *Gracián y la imaginación arquitectónica*. $28.00
24. Gloria Gálvez Lira, *Maria Luisa Bombal: realidad y fantasía*. $28.50
25. Susana Hernández Araico, *Ironía y tragedia en Calderón*. $25.00
26. Philip J. Spartano, *Giacomo Zanella: Poet, Essayist, and Critic of the "Risorgimento."* Preface by Roberto Severino. $24.00
27. E. Kate Stewart, *Arthur Sherburne Hardy: Man of American Letters*. Preface by Louis Budd. $28.50
28. Giovanni Boccaccio, *The Decameron*. English Adaptation by Carmelo Gariano. $30.00
29. Giacomo A. Striuli, "Alienation in Giuseppe Berto". $26.50
30. Barbara Mujica, *Iberian Pastoral Characters*. Preface by Frederick A. de Armas. $33.00
31. Susan Niehoff McCrary, *"'El último godo' and the Dynamics of the Urdrama."* Preface by John E. Keller. $27.50
32. *En torno al hombre y a sus monstruos: ensayos críticos sobre la novelística de Carlos Rojas*, editados por Cecilia Castro Lee y C. Christopher Soufas, Jr. $31.50
33. J. Thomas O'Connell, *Mount Zion Field*. $24.50
34. Francisco Delicado, *Portrait of Lozana: The Lusty Andalusian Woman*. Translation, introduction and notes by Bruno M. Damiani. $45.50
35. Elizabeth Sullam, *Out of Bounds*. Foreword by Michael G. Cooke. $23.50
36. Sergio Corsi, *Il "modus digressivus" nella "Divina Commedia."* $28.75
37. Juan Bautista Avalle-Arce, *Lecturas (Del temprano Renacimiento a Valle Inclán)*. $28.50
38. Rosendo Díaz-Peterson, *Las novelas de Unamuno*. Prólogo de Antonio Carreño. $30.00
39. Jeanne Ambrose, *Syntaxe Comparative Français-Anglais*. $29.50
40. Nancy Marino, *La serranilla española: notas para su historia e interpretación*. $28.75.
41. Carolyn Kreiter-Kurylo, *Contrary Visions*. Preface by Peter Klappert. $24.50
42. Giorgio Perissinotto, *Reconquista y literatura medieval: cuatro ensayos*. $29.50
43. Rick Wilson, *Between a Rock and a Heart Place*. $25.00
44. *Feminine Concerns in Contemporary Spanish Fiction by Women*. Edited by Roberto C. Manteiga, Carolyn Galerstein and Kathleen McNerney. $35.00
45. Pierre L. Ullman, *A Contrapuntal Method For Analyzing Spanish Literature*. $41.50

BOOK ORDERS

* Clothbound. *All book orders, except library orders, must be prepaid and addressed to **Scripta Humanistica**, 1383 Kersey Lane, Potomac, Maryland 20854. Manuscripts to be considered for publication should be sent to the same address.*